CONTENTS

P R E F A C E

How to Write First-Class Letters is designed to provide quick answers to your questions about writing effective letters. You simply find the chapter that covers what you need to know—there's no need to search through the entire book to find what you want.

In an informal, direct style, this book shows you how to compose a letter that communicates rather than merely informs. You will learn how to put your feelings, concerns, and needs into clear, effective words whether writing to friends, elected officials, businesses, or others. Model letters provide examples that you can adapt to your own circumstances.

HOW TO WRITE GREAT LETTERS

Part One of the book focuses on how to start a letter, organize it, and produce it in final form.

Chapter 1: It's Easier Than You Think presents the four questions that every letter must answer. Once you learn this simple technique you will always know how to start writing. The chapter also covers how to use tone, simplicity, and clarity to get your message across. The last section provides guidelines on when *not* to send a letter.

Chapter 2: Writing and Organizing Your Letters shows you how to break down any letter-writing process into three steps: prewriting, writing, and revising. Simple letter formulas help you organize your message so that the recipient understands why you are writing and what you want.

Chapter 3: Producing Your Letters provides guidelines on correct format and giving your message the best appearance.

Chapter 4: How To Address Just About Anyone shows you the correct forms of address for social titles; company, government, and court officials; diplomatic representatives; college and university officials; and religious and military orders.

SPECIAL FEATURES OF THIS BOOK

In addition to writing tips and model letters, the book provides appendixes containing postal abbreviations, easily confused words, and frequently misspelled words. This handy reference section can help you choose the right words and make sure your message is delivered quickly. In addition, a detailed index makes it easy to find the model letter you need or style question you want answered.

How to Write First-Class Letters, with its easy techniques, model letters, and appendixes, can help you "put it in writing."

MODEL LETTERS FOR NEARLY EVERY OCCASION

Part Two provides model letters for the many roles you play in life: family member, friend, consumer, citizen, and employee. Letter-writing tips in each chapter help you get the best results with your message.

Chapter 5: Social Letters covers a wide variety of social situations from announcements to sympathy notes to weddings. Social letters help you maintain good communication with friends and family and can serve as a form of dialogue with those who may live far away.

Chapter 6: Consumer Action Letters enhances your effectiveness as a consumer of goods and services. Letters in this chapter show you how to stand up for your rights, obtain information, and get an adjustment or refund for inadequate products and services.

Chapter 7: Civic Concerns deals with your role as a member of your community, state, and country. These model letters illustrate how to make your concerns and needs known to elected officials, school officials, religious leaders, the media, your neighbors, and volunteer organizations.

Chapter 8: Employment Letters helps you seek out and land that ideal job by showing you how to apply for a position, follow up on interviews, ask for or write recommendations, accept or refuse a job offer, and resign from a job. Good letter-writing skills can be an invaluable asset to your career life.

Chapter 9: Children's Letters deals with letters that children should know how to write. This chapter provides easy tips for teaching your children letter-writing skills from an early age.

HOW TO WRITE
GREAT LETTERS

CHAPTER
≡ONE

IT'S EASIER
THAN YOU THINK

Do any of these sound familiar?

▶ "Aunt Gail sent me that gift months ago. I'm too embarrassed to write a thank-you letter now, but I've got to say something."

▶ "Julia's husband died. I'd like to write her, but what do I say?"

▶ "How do you turn down an invitation to a shower without offending people?"

▶ "The lawnmower is broken again! One of these days that company is going to get a nasty letter from me."

▶ "What do I include in a letter of recommendation?"

▶ "If I knew who to write to in Washington, D.C., boy, would they get an earful from me on this tax issue!"

How many times have you wanted to write a letter but failed to do so because you didn't know what to say or whom to address? Practical letter writing is not only a social skill; it's a way of keeping the lines of communication between you and others in good working order. And it's an effective way to stand up for your rights when dealing with companies, service people, politicians, or others.

Even if English was your worst subject in school, you can learn to write clear, concise, effective letters. You would be amazed at the results you can achieve with a well-written message, whether to friends and family, colleagues, companies, politicians, or governments.

This chapter shows you where to start, how to use the key elements of tone, simplicity, and clarity in your letter, and when *not* to write a letter. (Guidelines for writing specific letters are given in each chapter in Part Two.)

Your objective is to write letters that *communicate* rather than simply *inform*. By breaking down the task into manageable steps, you'll discover that the art of skillful letter writing is easier than you think.

LETTER WRITING—A THREE-STEP PROCESS

Although letter writing involves only one person as writer, it is still a form of dialogue. You have something to say, and you want someone to receive, understand, and respond to your message.

To this end, you need to make your letters *recipient*-based rather than simply *writer*-based. That is, you must consider not merely your own interests and purposes but the needs, concerns, and abilities of the person to whom you are writing. Compare the two samples below:

Writer-Based Letter

Dear Senator Howells:

I thought I had heard it all, but when I caught your speech on Medicare, I could see I was wrong. I've never heard such clap-trap in my life—you obviously don't have any idea of the financial state of most senior citizens. I'll be happy to send you a copy of my monthly budget so you can get familiar with the real world out here. If you don't vote against cuts in Medicare, I'm voting against *you*!

Recipient-Based Letter

Dear Senator Howells:

On March 3, I happened to hear your speech on Medicare given before the Philadelphia Chamber of Commerce. Although you made several good points about the system's shortcomings, I was appalled to hear you advocate such steep cutbacks in third-party coverage. The National Health Consumer's recent study shows that most senior citizens would be severely hurt by such cutbacks. You have always been a strong advocate for senior citizens' benefits. Don't spoil your record now—vote against cuts in Medicare. We seniors need to feel we still have a good friend in the Senate.

The first letter parades the writer's feelings but fails to state the issue specifically or to acknowledge the recipient's achievements, past record, or overall stand on the issue. The ratio of "I" to "you" is overwhelming. The writer makes no attempt to communicate, only to sound off.

The second letter, while also stating the writer's feelings, does far more. It recognizes the recipient's worth, states the issue specifically, mentions supporting information likely to catch the recipient's attention, and closes by appealing to the recipient's image as a good friend of senior citizens. The ratio of "you" to "I" is the reverse of the first letter.

A simple three-step process—prewriting, writing, and revising—can help you create reader-based letters that communicate effectively.

▶ *Prewriting*—this step involves answering the four key questions of letter writing: What is my purpose? Who is my audience? What should the letter cover? What action or response do I want? Gather any pertinent information you may need to write your letter.

▶ *Writing*—in this step you write your rough copy all the way through to the end. Remember, *your first draft is a working draft.* Don't worry about phrasing, grammar, spelling, or organization at this point. Just write until you have a complete letter.

▶ *Revising*—read over your rough draft and organize your letter so that it flows logically from point to point. Check for grammar and spelling mistakes; double-check the accuracy of dates, facts, names, and figures; eliminate unnecessary words and irrelevant ideas; and proofread your final copy.

These three steps can help you get started and keep writing until you have a finished letter. Using this technique you should never again find yourself at a loss when you need to put your thoughts in writing.

WHERE TO START—FOUR KEY QUESTIONS

Most people put off letter writing because they don't know how to begin. Yet the process is remarkably easy if you keep in mind that all letters—formal or informal, social or business—must answer four key questions:

► What is the purpose of my letter—why am I writing it?

► Who am I writing to—who will receive the letter?

► What should I say about this subject—what do people *need* to know versus what is simply *nice* for them to know?

► What response or action do I want from the recipient—OR What key point(s) do I want the recipient to remember?

Once you know the answers to these questions, your letter is halfway written.

What Is the Purpose of My Letter?

The answer may be as simple as "I want to keep in touch with a friend," "I want to invite people to my son's wedding," "I want to welcome a new minister to our church," or as complex as "I want to describe why the new social security bill will cost taxpayers too much." Try to jot down your purpose in a sentence or two.

If you have trouble identifying exactly why you are writing to someone, talk the subject over with another person. Often the act of verbalizing what you want to say can clarify your purpose.

Who Am I Writing To?

Once you have identified your purpose, you need to consider the needs and characteristics of your intended readers. Are you writing to family, friends, business associates, club members, professional people, politicians? What are their concerns likely to be? What would they like or need to know about the subject of your letter? You might write very different letters on the same subject depending on who is your audience.

For example, suppose you want to start a new day-care center in your home. You write to your family, expressing your personal feelings about the project, how you have wanted to operate a day-care center ever since you were in high school, how excited you are about the prospect of going into business for yourself. The letter might look, in part, like the following:

> I can't believe I'm actually going to start my own business! After all these years of dreaming and planning, I just had to share this moment with you. I wanted you to know that all those years of putting up with my babysitting charges running through our house have paid off at last.

Now you have to write a letter to the city applying for a license to run a day-care institution. Your audience is not going to be interested in your personal excitement so much as your professional qualifications and experience. Your letter to city officials might look in part like this:

> I graduated from Baylor University with a BA degree in elementary education and an MA in special education. Since 1983 I have worked in the San Tomas County day-care center, first as a volunteer, then as paid staff supervising three volunteers. I speak fluent Spanish and conversational Vietnamese.

Finally, suppose you are writing to a foundation to apply for grant money to help fund your day-care center. This audience will want to know not only your professional qualifications but your financial status and plans. Your letter to them might read in part:

> We estimate first-year start-up costs to be $145,000 to cover basic expenses of rent, office space, supplies and equipment, staff, and incidentals. Thereafter, operating costs are estimated at $135,000 per year. See the attached financial statement for a detailed breakdown of all expensed items.

Take time to consider the needs and characteristics of your readers before you start writing. Ask yourself the following questions.

1. *Who is the intended recipient of my letter?* Have someone clearly in mind before you begin writing. Direct your letter to that person. The more accurately you can visualize your reader the more precisely you can tailor your message to get the results you want.

2. *What is the recipient's position and authority?* For example, if you want to complain about a product, does the person you are writing have the authority to act? If not, can you find out who does in the company? Or, if you are writing family members to help organize a reunion, who is likely to have the best organizing skills? Who would be more comfortable with a supporting role?

3. *Do you need to acknowledge the recipient's age, gender, nationality, or other personal characteristics?* In some instances, it may be appropriate to take into consideration your reader's personal characteristics when writing a letter. Acknowledging personal characteristics can be as simple as realizing that the deteriorating eyesight of an aging parent or relative makes it harder for him or her to read letters. You might want to write larger or type your letters so they are easier for the person to read.

    Attention to such details can make your letters more effective—and more appreciated.

4. *How much or how little does the recipient know about the subject of your letter?* What is the recipient's level of knowledge or skill regarding the subject? You want to avoid the twin traps of talking over the person's head or talking down to him or her.

    Your letter home explaining your job as a systems analyst, for example, should contain clear, nontechnical descriptions of the equipment and tools you use—unless you come from a family of systems analysts. On the other hand, a letter describing your job to a friend who is also an analyst can be written on a more technical level.

When you are writing to civic officials, politicians, school board members, or others, try to learn something about their level of expertise. Otherwise, you may overstate or understate your case and alienate your readers.

5. *What motivates the recipient?* The art of writing effective letters involves knowing something about what motivates people. This fact is particularly true if you are writing to persuade someone to do something for you. Can you appeal to his or her sense of security, prestige, or loyalty?

If you can identify the recipient's motivations, you have a better chance of gaining his or her attention and cooperation. You are creating *recipient*-based instead of *writer*-based communication. Your letter shows that you are sensitive to your reader's interests and concerns—not simply to your own. Remember, the object of writing a letter is to *communicate*. The more you consider others' needs, the better your chances of communicating successfully.

What Do I Need to Cover in My Letter?

Identifying your purpose and who you are writing to should help you determine what you need to cover in your letter. In effect, you are choosing what you will talk about from a whole range of facts. For example, if you want to urge the city to put up a stop sign at your street corner, you don't want to start out by discussing a history of stop signs or mentioning why every stop sign has been placed where it is in the city. You want to talk about why a stop sign is important for *your* corner.

By doing so, you take a broad topic—stop signs and safety—and draw a circle around only what you need to discuss in your letter, as shown in Figure 1.1. You are separating what your recipient *needs* to know from what is simply *nice* to know.

This principle is also appropriate for personal and social letters. Suppose you are writing to several friends, breaking the news to them that you and your spouse are separating. At this point, do you really need to tell them all the details? Would it be better simply to state the facts—you and your spouse have agreed to a trial separation to work out your differences—and let it go at that? Asking such questions gives you a chance to think things through before you write.

In many cases, telling all the facts is not the best choice. Saying only what really needs to be said may be a wiser course of action. You can always fill in more details later.

Figure 1.1 Focusing Your Topic

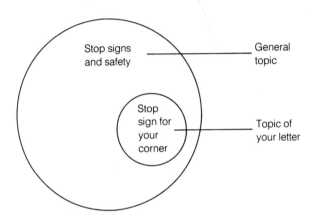

What Response or Action? What Important Facts?

The final question your letter must answer is what specific action or response you want from the recipient or what important facts you want the recipient to remember. Jot down the main points in a sentence or two so they are clear in your own mind.

If you want a particular action or response, state it clearly at the end of the letter. For example, if you are complaining about a defective product, do you want the recipient to refund your money, replace the item, or repair it free of charge? If you are sending an invitation, do you want the recipient to RSVP, respond only if they can't come, bring a gift, *not* bring a gift? Never assume the reader will know what you want just by reading the first part of your letter. Mind reading is not part of the communication process. Be specific about the action or response you want the reader to provide.

If you are simply sharing information, repeat the essential points in the last paragraph for the recipient's benefit. This simple technique can help your letter succeed as good communication.

STRIKE THE RIGHT TONE

Tone is one way you adapt your letters to different occasions and different readers. Tone refers to the emotional content of your letters. You can use a formal or informal, negative, positive, argumentative, or humorous tone. Each tone has its uses, although the negative and argumentative ones must be handled with sensitivity and care.

For instance, an informal tone is appropriate if you are inviting friends to a casual dinner, but a black-tie occasion requires a more formal tone.

Informal

Dear Robert and Jane,

Jerry and I are throwing a party Friday, May 13, to celebrate the Wildcats' regional conference victory. After 25 years we're in the playoffs! We would love to see the two of you there—just bring yourselves and your favorite Wildcat story. Dinner will be around 7:00. Come early and stay late!

Formal

Dear Mr. and Mrs. Jordan,

The Chancellor of the University is pleased to invite you and a guest to the annual University Alumni Dinner on Friday, May 13, 7:00 P.M., at Fisk Hall, 730 N. Windmeir Blvd. We have a special reason to celebrate this year as our football team has made the playoffs for the first time in 25 years.

Please respond by May 6 if you plan to attend. We look forward to the pleasure of your company.

The following guidelines will help you choose the right tone for the right occasion and audience.

Be Sincere

Avoid being too brusque or too gushy. Sincerity involves not only the honest expression of your thoughts and feelings but a sensitive regard for your recipient's situation as well. Whether you are writing to complain about something or to express your appreciation, avoid the extremes of insulting or flattering your reader. Readers are offended by the first approach and mistrust the second. If you have a legitimate complaint, state it clearly without berating the recipient.

Avoid:

Dear Julia,

When are you going to return my books? I loaned them to you three weeks ago—does it take you that long to read something? Please send them back immediately.

(With such a harsh, demanding tone, the writer will be lucky if her books are sent back in this century—plus the writer gives the reader no reason and no deadline to return the books.)

Better:

Dear Julia,

I hope you enjoyed the books you borrowed from me three weeks ago. They are among my favorite stories. Alice would like to borrow them next—could you return them to me by this Wednesday?
Thanks!

(The writer stresses the importance of the books to her, gives a reason and a date for their return, and thanks the reader for co-operating.)

Likewise, when expressing your appreciation, be specific about what you liked rather than simply throwing in a lot of sentimental words.

Avoid:

Dear Aunt Gail,

It was absolutely marvelous to see you and Uncle Paul! You are both fabulous people, I can't tell you how fantastic it was to spend an evening with you. We have to do it again soon! Thank you, thank you for a wonderful, wonderful time.

(This letter says nothing specific about what the writer liked or about what the recipient did to warrant appreciation—it simply serves as an emotional discharge for the writer.)

Better:

Dear Aunt Gail,

Thanks so much for treating us to dinner last night. Picking out a Thai restaurant was perfect, as Carl is fascinated by the Far East. I wish we had had more time to talk—your trip to Peru seems to have made a deep impression on you both. We'll have to make another date to finish the stories. Thank you again for your thoughtfulness and generosity.

(This letter is recipient-based, pointing out the actions and qualities the writer appreciated, and noting a major interest the reader expressed during the meal.)

Rather than allowing emotion to write your letters, think about what the recipient might want to hear. Emotion should serve as the spice in your message and not as the main course.

Keep It Positive

Use a positive tone when you must mention bad news—a refusal, rejection, or delay. No one likes to be turned down, or to have to turn down or disappoint someone else. When you must say ''no'' or in some way disappoint someone, maintain a positive tone. Don't mention the bad news in the first line. Instead, establish some common ground between you and the recipient, explain the reason for your decision or situation, and then state the decision. Develop the *you* attitude that puts the recipient's interests first. This principle works just as well for family or friends as for business or more formal occasions. Notice the difference in the samples:

Poor:

Sorry, but we can't come to your daughter's christening . . . .

Better:

Thanks so much for inviting us to Kelley's christening—we felt honored to be included. Unfortunately, we will be in New York that weekend helping my sister and her husband move into their new home. I'm truly sorry we won't be able to attend your daughter's christening . . . .

Poor:

I can't be scoutmaster this year . . . .

Better:

I was surprised and pleased to be nominated for scoutmaster this year—I know this is a position of considerable trust. However, my new position as Sales Director at work means I will be traveling much of the time and will be unable to attend most scout meetings. Therefore, with regret I must decline the nomination. I would be able to host a meeting or two, however, once the year's schedule is set . . . .

Try to emphasize what is positive in the situation and suggest an alternative course of action. If you can't attend an event or grant a request, suggest another way you might get together or some other favor you might grant. This technique softens the rejection and lets the reader know there will be other times when you will be able to say "yes." If the situation is such that you don't wish to extend this courtesy, at least soften the bad news in your letter by using a positive tone.

Keep It Personal

In this world of computerized communication and form letters to "occupant," it is important to retain the personal touch in your correspondence. Personal touches can range from the simple—including

a handwritten note with a formal invitation—to the more elaborate—
writing a friend's son or daughter to congratulate him or her on a personal achievement. Other ways you can put the personal touch in
your letter writing include:

> ▶ When you receive a gift or item in the mail from friends or rel-
> atives, send a short note or postcard right away telling them
> the items arrived and that you will write more later. At least
> you have let the sender know the items made it through the
> mail system safely. You won't have to waste time and energy
> feeling guilty for not writing a thank-you letter, and the sender
> won't have to wonder if the item fell off a mail truck and is ly-
> ing on the side of a highway.

> ▶ When responding to someone's letter, have the letter on hand
> so you can refer to items in the message. Nothing enhances
> your letter so much as mentioning something important to the
> recipients or answering questions they asked in their letter to
> you. If they were preparing for a difficult speech, going on va-
> cation, sending their first child off to college—ask them how it
> went, how are they doing? If they want to know what's hap-
> pening in your life, you can respond specifically to their con-
> cerns. This technique is part of maintaining a written dialogue
> with your correspondents.

> ▶ When sending commercially printed cards for birthdays, wed-
> dings, graduations, and so on, add your own personal wishes
> in addition to the printed message. Even brief comments like
> "May this be the best birthday ever!" or "I wish we could cel-
> ebrate together—Happy Birthday" add warmth and personality
> to the card. You don't have to outdo the printed message—just
> add your own sincere thoughts.

> ▶ Acknowledge good work wherever you encounter it. It's a
> well-known fact that people are ten times more likely to put
> their complaints in writing rather than their compliments. If a
> grocery clerk helped you find your child lost in the store, a
> salesperson made an extra effort on your behalf, a physician
> spent more time with you to explain a difficult procedure—

why not let them know you appreciated it? The message needn't be elaborate—you can even write a brief note on the bill when you pay it. "Thanks for your help," "Thanks for talking with me"—a short phrase can do the job.

► Include a brief note with any gifts or material you send to people. Even a simple "Dear Jim, Here it is. Regards Mark" is better than no note at all. People like to feel someone took the time to personalize their correspondence.

Knowing how to use various tones and how to maintain the personal touch in your correspondence is a valuable letter-writing skill.

MAKE IT SIMPLE AND CLEAR

Many people feel that their written correspondence should be more "official" sounding than their conversation. They throw in two-dollar words; stiff, awkward phrasing; and formal expressions to make their message appear more important. They end up losing their own natural "voice" and generally confusing their recipients. They might say, "Herewith find enclosed the materials per your request April 12" when they mean, "Enclosed are the materials you wanted."

Writing can be as natural as speaking. The best way to simplify your language and retain your own voice is to challenge your writing with the question, "Is there a simpler, clearer way to say this?" The following guidelines for brevity and clarity will help you streamline your messages and communicate your ideas more effectively.

Brevity

Brevity, it has been said, is the soul of wit. But most people have acquired wordy expressions that they use without thinking. These expressions overburden their letters and obscure their message. By paying more attention to your language, you can eliminate this unwanted baggage from your letters.

1. *Substitute more concise wording for unnecessary words and phrases.* Listed below are some of the most common wordy phrases people use in letters. Compare them to their more precise alternatives. Substitute the more concise version in your own writing whenever you find yourself using a wordy phrase.

Wordy	*Concise*
blue in color	blue ("blue" *is* a color)
at this point in time	at this time
consensus of opinion	consensus
meet together	meet (implies "together")
during the course of	during
few in number	few
personal in manner	personal
in the vast majority of cases	in most cases
on a weekly basis	weekly
the month of March	March
square in shape	square (means "shape")
until such time as	until
at a time when	when
with the exception of	except
prior to	before
due to the fact that	because
in spite of the fact that	in spite of
very necessary	necessary
on a practical basis	practically

2. *Use adjectives and adverbs sparingly.* A well-placed adverb or adjective can add interest and color to your letters. Too many modifiers, however, weaken your meaning and give your message an insincere, exaggerated tone.

   Poor:

   Your gift was *absolutely, positively fabulous.* I think it's the *most unique* circle pin I've ever received—and I mean *ever.* It's *heavenly, divine, completely wonderful!*

Better:

The circle pin is *beautiful.* I love the way the gold braid stands out. Thank you so much for your *lovely* gift; it will get a lot of wear.

3. *Avoid the phrases "there is" and "there are"; use more active verbs.* The phrases "there is" and "there are" add nothing to your letters. Whenever possible, rewrite your sentences to use stronger, more active verbs.

Poor:

There are always other times we can meet.

Better:

We can always *find* other times to meet.

Poor:

There is something I have to tell you.

Better:

I *need* to tell you something. *OR* I *have* something to tell you.

4. *Try to condense or eliminate expressions beginning with which, that, or who.* Look for these phrases and clauses in your letters and revise them wherever you can.

Poor:

The speaker, *who was from Talman Savings,* gave a talk *that was overly long but interesting.*

Better:

The *Talman Savings* speaker gave a *lengthy but interesting* talk.

Poor:

The novel, *which is written in three parts,* told a story *that took place in the Middle Ages.*

Better:

The *three-part* novel told a story *set in the Middle Ages.*

Clarity

Clear writing involves choosing the best words to express your ideas. The meaning of a word depends on the context in which it is used and the understanding of the person who uses it. Keep the following points in mind to help you get the words just right.

1. *Keep your language vivid and concrete.* The more clichés, slang, and abstract words you use, the less clear your message. Be especially on guard against clichés—tired, overworked phrases that say nothing of substance—and slang—popular expressions that quickly become outmoded. These terms and expressions come easily to mind because you hear them often. Eliminate them in your own writing and state what you mean in your own words.

   Poor:

   I guess you know that Bill is the *head honcho* at his job now. He's responsible for making sure everyone *toes the line. It's plain as the nose on your face* that he's got ambitions—*the bottom line* for him has always been rising to the *top of the heap.*

   (The slang and clichés appear to say something, but actually leave much unsaid. What exactly is Bill's position? What does he do? What are his ambitions?)

   Better:

   I guess you know that Bill has been promoted to Vice President, Sales. He's responsible for supervising the activities of 24 salespeople. Bill has always been ambitious—one of the major goals in his life has been to be a vice president or even president of a company.

   (The reader now knows much more specific information about Bill than was conveyed in the previous letter.)

2. *Emphasize the active over the passive voice.* The active voice stresses who or what *did* or *is* something (I *bought* the car). The passive voice emphasizes who or what *receives* the action (The car *was bought* by me). The active voice is a more vivid, lively form to use in your letters. Compare the two samples below.

Passive:

The game *was won* in the last second.

Active:

Our team *won* the game in the last second.

Notice how the active voice brings the actors back into the picture and enlivens the entire message. The only instance in which the passive voice may be preferred is when you wish to establish a neutral tone before launching into your main point.

Diplomatic Passive:

You asked me to give you an estimate for how much it would cost to replace the ebony lamp that *was broken* last weekend.

(No need to say the reader's youngest child broke the lamp.)

Active:

If you like, you *can pay* the manufacturer directly or *wait* until the lamp arrives here. . . .

(The active voice brings the reader back into the letter.)

In general, use the active voice in your correspondence; save the passive voice for occasions when you need to be diplomatic.

3. *Keep your references clear.* When you use words to modify or refer to other words, make sure the recipient can follow your train of thought. You may provide some unintended humor if you are careless about your references.

Unclear:

I'll send my son to pick you up at the airport. He'll be the sandy-haired boy driving a white Chevy named Carl.

Clear:

I'll send my son, Carl, to pick you up at the airport. Look for a sandy-haired boy driving a white Chevy.

Make sure you keep your subject and verb together. This arrangement helps clarify your thoughts.

Poor:

The *canyon,* which the park rangers told us has the longest stretch of rapids in the world and whose temperature varies by as much as eighty degrees from top to bottom, *is* a spectacular sight.

Better:

The *canyon is* a spectacular sight. The park rangers told us it has the longest stretch of rapids in the world. Did you know that the temperature from top to bottom varies nearly eighty degrees?

Finally, be careful that your references are correct. Words such as *this, that, which,* **and** *it* **should refer to specific ideas or nouns in the preceding sentence. Study the examples below. Correct any errors in your own writing.**

Unclear:

I served avocados at lunch, *which* no one felt like eating.

(Is it the lunch or the avocados no one felt like eating?)

Clear:

No one felt like eating the avocados I served at lunch.

Unclear:

The secretary couldn't answer my questions, and the sales manager was rude. *This* can cost you customers.

(*This* refers to the entire sentence—is it the employees or their behavior that are being objected to?)

Clear:

The secretary couldn't answer my questions, and the sales manager was rude. Such *poor service* has cost Erhardt another customer—me!

You can use a variety of methods to correct confusing references: Break one sentence into two or more sentences, restate the sentence, rearrange word order, or fill in the missing reference.

WHEN *NOT* TO SEND A LETTER

So far, this chapter has discussed the best way to express yourself in a letter. But at times, *not* sending a letter can be a master stroke on your part. The communication process may be served better if you think before you write. Ask yourself the following questions.

1. *Is writing a letter the best way to handle this matter?* In some cases, calling or talking to the person face to face may be a better way to communicate than through a letter. This fact is particularly true if you need a response right away or want the opportunity to ask and answer questions. Asking a favor, settling a disagreement, straightening out a misunderstanding, or discussing sensitive situations may be handled best by talking things over in person.

2. *Do I have all the facts I need to write a letter?* Nothing is more embarrassing than to fire off an angry letter about something only to find that you misunderstood the situation or missed a key fact. No one likes looking foolish. Save yourself embar-

rassment and needless trouble by checking your facts before you write. If you heard a school board member wants to censor certain books, make sure you have the story straight before writing the superintendent of schools or your local public officials.

Also, ask yourself if you really need to take action at all. If your daughter and son-in-law are having difficulties, for example, do you really need to write each one offering your advice? It might be better to wait and see what happens. In some cases, the dispute may be settled best by the parties involved.

Take time to be sure of your facts before you commit yourself on paper. The written word is difficult to take back.

3. *Am I too emotional to write the best letter?* In general, it's best not to send a letter written in anger. While it may provide you with immediate satisfaction, the long-term loss of goodwill and damage to relationships that can result is seldom worth the price.

If you find yourself too emotionally charged, take a walk, talk the situation over with someone, or write the letter *but don't send it.* Find some way to work off your emotions. Once your head is cooler, think about what you want to say. The end result may be far different—and more effective—than your first message, yet still preserve your integrity.

Keep in mind that your goal is to *communicate,* not simply to discharge your emotions. To write effective communication, your mind has to play a major role in what you say and how you say it.

The next chapter discusses how to write and organize your letters using various letter formulas. By selecting the appropriate formula, you can quickly organize any letter.

CHAPTER
≡Two

Writing and ORGANIZING YOUR LETTERS

Most people have little trouble writing social letters to friends and family that convey general news. But when they must write a letter with a specific purpose—to straighten out a computer error on a bill, complain about poor city service, describe an accident for an insurance claim—they are likely to experience a moment of panic. Where to start? How to write the letter? How to get results?

This chapter looks at the parts of a letter and the three-step process of prewriting, writing, and revising your message.

PARTS OF A LETTER

Most letters have many or all of the following basic parts, depending on the letter's purpose and intended audience. Whether you handwrite or type your letters, these basic parts remain the same.

Personalized Letterhead
Dateline (month, day, year)
Heading and Inside Address (for more formal letters)
Salutation
Body (opening, middle, closing paragraphs)
Complimentary Close
Signature
Postscript, Enclosures, Copies

The parts of a letter are discussed in more detail in ''Chapter 3: Producing Your Letters.''

Personalized Letterhead

Personalized stationery may consist of no more than your initials or may include your full name and address, as shown in Figure 2.1. The variety of type styles and papers gives you a wide range of choices from strictly formal to artistic to humorous. Many people like to reveal their personality through their stationery. Make sure, however, that your letterhead is appropriate to the occasion. If you send a letter of complaint on humorous stationery, chances are the reader will have trouble taking you seriously.

Figure 2.1 Samples of Personal Letterhead

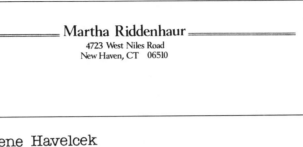

Dateline

It's a good idea to date your letters—even your social correspondence. You might want to refer to the letter at a later time, and it will be helpful to know when you wrote it. All letters that are sent to companies, government agencies or officials, public officials, and the like should be dated. These letters can serve as written documentation of your correspondence.

Heading and Inside Address

If you do not have personalized stationery, you will need to add a heading. This is simply your own address handwritten or typed single space two lines below the dateline and two lines above the salutation, as shown below:

July 12, 19--

1234 Riverton Lane
Apt. 3W
Tuscaloosa, AL 23345

Dear Guyetta,

Your more formal correspondence—to public officials, professional service people, or corporate management—will require an inside address. The inside address is typed below the dateline, single spaced, and flush with the left margin. It contains the reader's name, title (if any), company division or department or civic agency, mailing address, and ZIP code of the receiver.

James T. Farrell   Cynthia B. Lewis
Senior Partner   Public Affairs Director
Barrows, Farrell, & Yarby, Inc.   Health and Human Services
One East Madison   139 West Division   Room 6
Chicago, IL 60603   Ripon, WI 54971

Salutation

The salutation is typed two lines down from the inside address, flush with the left margin. In informal correspondence, the salutation is followed by a comma. In formal letters, use a colon.

Dear Marge,   Dear Senator Dodge:

The correct forms of address used in salutations to people of various professions or for particular social occasions are described in more detail in "Chapter 4: How to Address Just About Anyone."

Body of the Letter

The body of the letter begins two lines down from the salutation. Paragraphs are typed single space with double spaces between them. Depending on the letter format you use, you can either indent the first line of each paragraph or type it flush with the left margin. ''Chapter 3: Producing Your Letters'' provides examples of letter formats: block, full-block, semiblock, and simplified.

It is best, even in short letters, to divide the body into an opening, middle, and closing paragraph. These parts are discussed in more detail on pages 37–45. This step makes your letter easier to read and presents your message more clearly.

Complimentary Close

The complimentary close is typed two lines below the body of the letter. It can be centered on the page or typed flush with the left or right margin, depending on the letter format you choose. Complimentary closings can be formal (*Sincerely, Truly yours*) or informal (*Best wishes, Love, Warmest regards*).

Signature

In most social and informal correspondence, the writer signs his or her name after the complimentary closing. In more formal letters, you may want to type your name four lines below the complimentary closing and sign your name in the space between. If you want to include your address and telephone number as well, place them below your typed name.

With warmest regards,

Vera Preston

Sincerely yours,

Vera Preston
Vera Preston
2113 Bluestone Drive
Hardin, NM 87973
(780) 331-4545

Postscript, Enclosures, Copies

The P.S., or postscript, line is typed two lines below the signature or last line of the writer's address or telephone number. This line is used for last-minute thoughts or for information mistakenly left out of the letter.

If you want to let the recipient know you have included material with your letter, you can use an enclosures line (written either *Encl:* or *Enclosures:*). This line is also typed one double space below the signature or last line of the address or telephone number.

Best wishes,

Vera Preston

P.S. Call me by Wednesday!

Truly yours,

Vera Preston

Vera Preston
2113 Bluestone Drive
Hardin, NM 87973
(780) 331-4545

Encl: Résumé and portfolio

In some cases, you will need to send copies of your letter to people other than your reader. Use the abbreviation *cc:* or *Copies:* and list those who will also receive your letter. The copies line is typed two lines below the signature or last line of the address or telephone number.

Vera Preston
2113 Bluestone Drive
Hardin, NM 87973
(780) 331-4545

cc: Abel Hardesty, President
Barbara Fisch, Director of Sales

PREWRITING

By keeping the three-step process in mind, you can overcome your fear of writing. Begin with the four key questions of the *prewriting stage*. Establish your purpose, your audience, the scope of your topic, and the response or action you want. Suppose, for example, that you want to make a change in your life insurance policy. Your answers to the four questions might look like the following:

Purpose:
To reduce the amount of life insurance coverage in my policy and the monthly premiums I have to pay

Who I'm Writing To:
Life insurance agent

Scope of Topic:
Explain the changes I want to make and how I want to set up the new policy

Action Desired:
I want the agent to make the changes, inform me when they have been accomplished, and send me a new policy along with payment schedule

If you need to do a little background research or collect materials to help you write, this is the time to gather your information. Once you have even preliminary answers to the four key questions, you are ready to write. During the writing, you may discover that you want to make changes in the purpose of your letter or in the action or response you want from the recipient. Even if this is the case, your initial answers give you a starting point for writing.

WRITING—THREE STRATEGIES TO GET STARTED

Many people get through the prewriting stages and still feel intimidated about actually writing the letter. You can get around this problem by using a few key writing strategies to help you start and keep on going until you finish the letter. The most helpful among these strategies are freewriting, laundry list, and mapping techniques.

Freewriting

The key to freewriting is to ignore the part of you that wants to revise or correct your words as you write. Simply start writing the first things that come into your mind about the subject. For the time being, forget about grammar, spelling, punctuation, organization, or format. All that can be added later. Pick up a pen or pencil, or get on the computer, and just write. Here's how your first try at the insurance letter might look using the freewriting technique.

> Want to cut back on expenses—reduce life insurance coverage to $20,000, monthly payments by half. Make it effective the first of the month. Parents now deceased, need to change beneficiary. Leaving business, don't need as much coverage. Probably make it my brother and his wife. Need Rhonda to change policy but keep automatic payment debit from checking account, also schedule of increases for the next five years—maybe talk about annuity this year. Have her send copy of new policy, ask about old—want it back? hold onto it? Like to have the same rider about accident insurance, never can tell what might happen.

You'll need to go back and revise your letter—the next section shows you how to organize your message. But you have created the rough draft. For most people, that means the hardest part is over.

Laundry List

The principle behind this technique is a brainstorming session, and all ideas are fair game. Simply jot down a list of items that come to mind, no matter how irrelevant or trivial they may seem. Don't judge or edit your thoughts—you can always eliminate ideas later. For now, set your mind free to create a list of ideas on your topic. A laundry list for the insurance letter might look like the following:

1. Want to cut back on expenses for next five years, do magazine writing

2. Reduce life insurance coverage, payments

3. Make it $20,000 or less, talk to Rhonda, effective first of the month

4. Have Rhonda change policy, beneficiary

5. Make beneficiary brother? Aunt Carla?

6. Keep automatic debit for payment

7. Need schedule of payment increases, new policy

8. Maybe talk about annuity, disability?

Your next step is to determine which items can be eliminated. For example, you may not want to talk about annuities and disability insurance in this letter but save the topic for another time.

Mapping

People who have trouble freewriting or generating lists often find that the mapping technique works best. Mapping is also known as "clustering" or "mind mapping." This technique takes advantage of the mind's natural ability to organize information.

Although there is no one correct way to do mapping, some general guidelines have proven effective.

1. Write the topic of your letter in the center of a piece of paper—for example, "policy changes."

2. Draw a circle around the term. This may seem like an odd step, but for some reason the mind likes to have visual boundaries around a subject.

3. Draw a line branching from the circle or square for every main item or idea you think of about your topic. Don't try to organize the branches, just let yourself develop them. Organizing comes later.

4. You can use different colored pens or pencils for different branches. Some people find that using different colors helps them to organize the letter after they finish the map.

Figure 2.2 shows how the mapping technique might work for the insurance policy letter.

You may find some surprises using this technique. Your conscious and unconscious mind together know far more than you generally realize. You may write down ideas or thoughts you didn't know you had. The advantage of this technique is that it engages all parts of the mind.

Figure 2.2 Mapping Technique

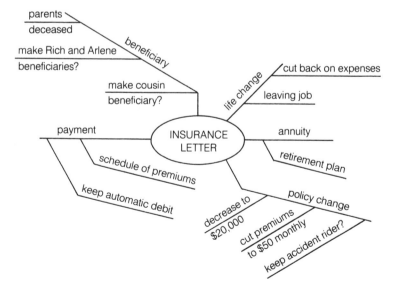

WRITING—ORGANIZING THE LETTER

Once you have generated your rough copy, list of ideas, or topic map, you are ready to organize your letter. You can use several letter formulas to organize your message, depending on the type of letter you need to write.

Organizing with Letter Formulas

Letter formulas enable you to tailor your letter to any situation. The most common letter formulas are described below, along with the most appropriate uses of each formula.

Inverted Pyramid Structure. When using the inverted pyramid structure, you state the most important point first—similar to a newspaper story. For example, you want to let relatives know that your child has won a scholarship to college. The rest of the letter elaborates on your main point, as shown in Figure 2.3. This formula is tailor-made for such correspondence as announcements; important news about family, friends, local events, and so on; and complaints or compliments. Your primary objective is to focus the recipient's attention on your main point in the first sentence or paragraph.

Figure 2.3 Inverted Pyramid Structure

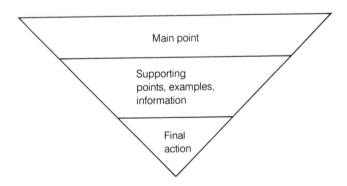

Diamond Sequence.   In contrast to the inverted pyramid structure, the diamond sequence is used to prepare the reader *before* you give your main point. This formula is best used when you have to say "no" to a request or invitation, when you need to ask the recipient for a favor, or when you must catch the recipient up on the history of a situation. As shown in Figure 2.4, the main point forms the midsection of the diamond shape.

Figure 2.4 Diamond Structure

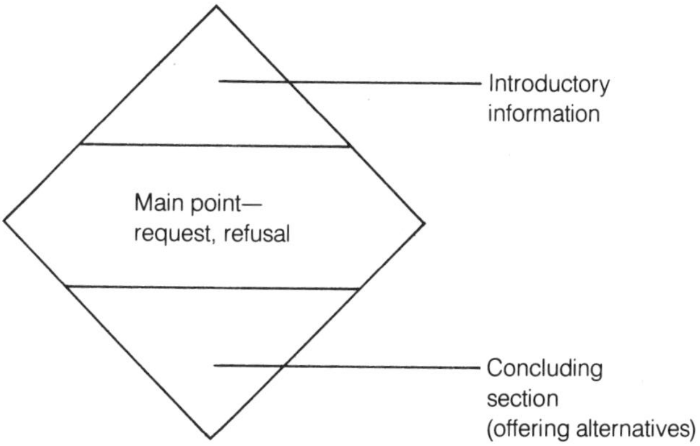

Introductory information

Main point—
request, refusal

Concluding section
(offering alternatives)

Problem-Solving Format.   The problem-solving format generally begins with a description of a problem or problems and ends with a discussion of solutions. Suppose, for instance, you had planned to host the family reunion but a fire damaged your home. You would explain your situation and suggest alternative sites for the reunion—a resort nearby, another relative's home, a hotel or motel in the area.

In another instance, you wish to register a complaint with a company about a product. You would state the problem and propose the solutions you wanted the company to consider or the solution you will accept.

The problem-solving formula is ideal for settling disputes, resolving problem situations, and for lodging complaints when you wish to propose a solution or to negotiate with the recipient.

Chronological Format. The chronological structure is used when you wish to describe the order of events as they took place. You can either start at the beginning and move forward in time, or state the end result and then go back to the beginning to show how the situation developed.

For instance, if you are describing how you broke your leg, you might begin by describing your trip to the mountains, how you decided to climb down a steep trail, and how you fell. The end result: a broken leg. Or you could begin by announcing you have a broken leg, then tell how it happened.

This format is the best choice when reporting on an event or situation that requires a blow-by-blow account of what happened. Accident reports to an insurance agent, descriptions of family events or vacation outings, or eyewitness accounts of a situation are all topics that lend themselves to a chronological formula.

Question-and-Answer Format. The question-and-answer formula is particularly useful when you must explain a procedure or give directions or instructions. Perhaps you must tell the recipient how to get to your house, how to use an item you have sent in the mail, how to fill out a form or follow a particular procedure (register to vote, renew a driver's license, challenge a credit card statement).

In this format, you ask yourself questions the recipient will want to know and you answer them in your letter. Before writing the letter, brainstorm a list of questions and answers, then arrange them in the most logical order.

The question-and-answer formula is the best choice for correspondence in which you must explain something step by step that you wish the recipient to do.

Ranking Topics

Once you have created a rough draft, list of ideas, or mapping—and selected the letter formula that best fits your topic—you are ready to rank your points in logical order.

If you have trouble identifying the main topic, ask yourself which item would you save if you could keep only one. In a description of a fire in your home, for instance, which is the most important point—the fact that everyone got out unhurt? that the house was or was not destroyed? that the fire was started by a faulty heater? Which point would you keep as the *main* idea?

Body of the Letter

Now you are ready to write the final version of your letter. The process can be broken down into manageable steps if you understand that every letter, regardless of its purpose or the formula used, can be divided into three parts—the opening, middle, and closing. Each part has a specific purpose.

Opening. The opening paragraph or sentences establish the purpose of your letter. The opening contains either the main point or, in some cases, important preliminary information. Since this section must catch and hold the recipient's attention, make sure that you use shorter, more varied sentences to express your message.

You can begin by freewriting your opening paragraph, then revising it. In general, the finished version should be no more than five or six sentences long. Compare the two examples below:

Freewriting:

Need to reduce expenses, so need to cut life insurance back to $20,000 and get monthly payments down to $50, and make this and other changes effective by first of month.

Revision:

Dear Rhonda:

I am making a career change in two months and must reduce my monthly expenses for a time. As a result, I would like to decrease my life insurance policy to $20,000 with a $50 monthly premium. Can you make this and other changes by the first of the month?

Notice that in the freewriting paragraph one idea crowds in on the heels of another. It's hard to absorb the purpose and intent of the letter. In the revised paragraph, however, the sentences are no more than seventeen to twenty words in length. The reader has time to grasp one idea before the next one is presented.

Modern language experts find that people understand information better when it is packaged in smaller bites. Although most people speak in concise sentences, when they put their thoughts in writing the length nearly doubles. This is not to say that all your sentences should be short or choppy. Instead, by following a few easy guidelines, you can break up your sentences or combine them to mimic the rhythms of natural speech.

1. *Include only one or two ideas in each sentence.* When a sentence contains more than one or two ideas, the writer appears to be free associating. Look over your sentences to see where you may be crowding three or more ideas into one sentence. Shorter sentences give you an opportunity to state your purpose and catch the recipient's interest right away.

2. *Watch for linking and connecting words to split or combine sentences.* If you tend to write long sentences, look for words like *and, but, which, while, because, although,* and *however* in your writing. They often indicate a natural break where you can divide long sentences into shorter ones.

Original:

Arlene thinks we can rent the cottage for under $150 and still get the deluxe cabin by the lake, *although* I think April is too early to go *because* the weather that far north is usually cold until late May or even early June.

Revised:

Arlene thinks we can rent the cottage for under $150 and still get the deluxe cabin by the lake. However, I think April is too early to go. The weather that far north is usually cold until late May or even early June.

If you tend to write short, choppy sentences, use connecting words like *however, consequently, although, but, because,* and *and* to combine sentences. You can also rewrite two sentences into one.

Original:

The Girl Scout troop is meeting Tuesday at 3:30. They are working on merit badges. They will work on them for three weeks. We will have a speaker for the meeting. She is Fran Booth from the Animal Shelter. She is a good speaker. She's worked with Girl Scout troops for many years.

Revised:

The Girl Scout troop is meeting Tuesday at 3:30. For the next three weeks, they will be working on merit badges. Our speaker for the meeting is Fran Booth from the Animal Shelter. She's a good speaker and has worked with Girl Scout troops for many years.

3. *Vary sentence structure.* When speaking, you pause between ideas, raise or lower your voice for emphasis, repeat key words or phrases, and use body language to add extra meaning and variety to your words. You can add some of this color to your writing simply by varying sentence structure. This technique imitates the tone and rhythms of natural speech and imparts a warmer, more conversational mood to your messages. When sentences are all the same structure, the letter can appear stuffy or monotonous.

Original:

By the way, we are running late in sending out our Christmas cards. *As a result,* you may get yours after Christmas. *Never fear,* we should get them to you by New Year's. *Wouldn't you know,* we even started early this year!

Revised:

By the way, we are running late in sending out our Christmas cards. You may get yours after Christmas but, we hope, before New Year's. Would you believe we even started early this year!

Often you can vary sentence structure merely by rearranging phrases or clauses within a sentence. For example:

When you get home, be sure to give us a call.
Be sure to give us a call *when you get home.*

You can also vary structure by rephrasing a sentence or breaking it into two sentences.

Marie tells me you'll be home on Wednesday, so call us when you get in and we'll get together.
Marie told me you'll be home on Wednesday. Call us when you get in, and we'll get together.

These simple guidelines can help you to write opening paragraphs that focus attention on your main point and encourage the recipients to read the rest of the letter.

Middle. The middle portion of a letter is used to support, explain, or elaborate on your main point. It is composed of a series of sentences or paragraphs that lead the recipient from one point or fact to another until the letter's closing. However, you don't want to create large blocks of text or one-sentence paragraphs that make it difficult for the recipient to understand your message.

A few well-tested techniques can highlight information and help you to organize and express your thoughts—and help the recipient grasp the message. These devices include using brief paragraphs, lists, and emphasis devices (capitalization, underscoring, and punctuation) to create the body of your letter.

Brief paragraphs. Your skill at writing shorter, more varied sentences will also help you create concise paragraphs. Although no hard-and-fast rules exist regarding the length of paragraphs, some general guidelines can help.

1. *Keep your paragraphs within five or seven sentences long.* Generally, if paragraphs are longer, they contain too many ideas and need to be split into two or more paragraphs.

2. *To determine where paragraph breaks should occur, notice how sentences group around your ideas.* In writing paragraphs, you present a topic, discuss it for a few sentences, then move on to the next topic. Sentences will tend to group naturally around these ideas. For example:

> Parents now deceased, need to change beneficiary. Probably make it my brother and his wife. Need Rhonda to keep automatic payment debit from checking account, also schedule of increases for the next five years—like to have the same rider about accident insurance, never can tell what might happen.

The sentences in this paragraph group around three topics: change in beneficiary, automatic payment and schedule of increases, and accident rider. You would break the text into shorter paragraphs to discuss these topics.

> Because both my parents are now deceased, I would like to change the beneficiary of my policy. Please fill in the names of my brother Charles Richmond and his wife Arlene Elizabeth as the new beneficiaries.
> Let's keep the same automatic payment arrangement with the new policy that we had with the old. I believe all you have to do is tell the bank how much is to be deducted each month from my checking account. If you can, send me a schedule of premium increases for the next five years. That way, I'll know how much more is being deducted each year.
> Will I be able to keep the same accident insurance rider?

My accountant seemed to think it was a good addition to the policy. Let me know if I have to apply for it again with the new policy.

3. *Discuss only one idea in a paragraph.* Make sure that each paragraph develops only one idea. In this way, you lead the recipient from one point to the next through the body of the letter. He or she can more easily follow your train of thought. This fact is particularly important if you are trying to persuade someone to grant your request, if you are arguing a point, or if you are describing events in chronological order.

Lists. Lists can make your letter easier to read and draw attention to important information. For instance, suppose you are writing a letter to let friends know when your plane arrives and departs. Compare the two examples below:

Original:
This is the first vacation we have had in six years, so we are really excited about coming out. Our flight arrives May 17 at 3:30 in the afternoon, American Airlines #578, which is the same day we all met six years ago! It's too bad we won't have longer to stay, but we have to leave May 23. Our departure time is seven o'clock in the evening on United Airlines #332. Anyway—I can't wait to see you!

Revised:
This is the first vacation we have had in six years, so we are really excited about coming out. I don't know if you remember, but May 17–23 are the exact dates we got together six years ago! Our flight information is:
Arrive: May 17, 3:30 P.M., American Airlines #578
Depart: May 23, 7:00 P.M., United Airlines #332
We can't wait to see you!

In the first version, the important information about arrival and departure times and dates is buried in a solid block of text. The revised version emphasizes the essential information and makes it easy for the recipient to pick out times and dates at a glance. The listing technique can greatly improve your chances of being met at the airport on the right day, at the right time.

A few words of caution about using lists. Number your lists if the sequence is important—steps in a procedure, for example. Also, use lists sparingly in your letters. They are meant to highlight information, not to convert all your paragraphs into numbered items.

Capitalization, underscoring, punctuation.   You can also highlight information and add variety to your letter by the selective use of capitalization, underscoring, and punctuation (dashes, colons, parentheses). The key word in this technique is *selective*. Too much of any of these devices dilutes the effect you want to make on the reader. Compare the two examples below:

Poor:

Last week I bought a PYLON WARRIOR computer game from your company. I can't believe—maybe I'm just naive or simple— but I can't believe the SHODDY quality of the game. I called your service tech three times trying to get the game (so-called) up on the computer. HOW CAN YOU SELL SUCH AWFUL MERCHANDISE?

(Overuse of underscoring, capitalization, and punctuation makes this letter sound like the work of a crank or chronic complainer. The company representative is likely to believe the person simply didn't know how to follow directions.)

Better:

Last week I bought a PYLON WARRIOR computer game from your company. Usually I have no trouble booting up your games, but this one wouldn't work. After calling your service tech three times, we both gave up. Please check your game program— obviously something is wrong. I've already returned PYLON WARRIOR for a full refund. Let's hope you can fix the problem: Up to now your company has had an excellent reputation.

(The selective use of capitalization, underscoring, and punctuation emphasizes the writer's problems without exaggerating them.)

Capitalization or underscoring can be used to call attention to names, places, particular wording (emphasizing *not* or *no*), or key information. However, you want to avoid the impression that you are shouting at the recipient or consider him or her too dumb to understand the message without considerable help from you. Keep in mind the element of tact in using capitalization or underscoring.

Likewise punctuation, used sparingly, can open your sentences and highlight important information. Dashes, for example, set off ideas or topics within a sentence.

> Everyone is coming—even Lorraine and Shuji—so we'll have a full house that week.

Colons, like dashes, set off information within a sentence. They break up the text visually and can be used to introduce a list.

Parentheses call attention to information within a paragraph but in a more subtle way. The parenthetical break should be brief. If you find yourself writing two or more sentences in parentheses, you probably should drop the parentheses and begin a new paragraph.

> Please send us a brochure on your holiday tours (weekends only) of the Merrimack River Canyon.

The skillful use of brief paragraphs, lists, and emphasis devices can greatly enhance your letters. Don't overuse them or throw them in arbitrarily. Their presence should strengthen and clarify your message, increasing its impact on the recipient.

Closing.   In the closing section of a letter, you let the recipient know what action or response you want or what important information should be emphasized. The closing can be a simple sentence, "Let me know which weekend, May 15–17 or May 22–24, is the best for you," or a paragraph restating the main points of your letter. Make sure the recipient knows clearly what you want or why you have written. Compare the two closing paragraphs below.

Poor:

The life insurance policy change is just the beginning of a lot of changes in my life. I'd appreciate your help in getting me launched on my new career.

(This closing doesn't repeat key information or tell the recipient what specific actions the writer wants taken.)

Better:

I'd like the new life insurance policy, complete with the changes discussed above, to take effect by the first of this month. If this is not possible, let me know and we can set a new date. Please send the new policy, along with a schedule of premium increases, to my current address. I appreciate your help in taking care of this matter.

(The writer has repeated key information and stated clearly what action the recipient should take.)

The nature of your closing depends on your purpose for writing. Reread your closing to be sure the recipient knows what action or response you want or what key information he or she should remember.

REVISING

The *revision stage* is your last chance to check your letter before mailing it out. The checklist below can help ensure that you have answered the four key questions, crafted your language, checked your grammar and your facts, and proofread the final version for typographical or other careless mistakes and errors.

Checklist for Review

► *Parts of the letter.* Make sure you have filled out the date, inside address (if needed), salutation, complimentary closing, and signature lines correctly. Is the name and address of your recipient accurate? Have you signed your letter? Do you need to add a postscript, enclosures, or copies line?

► *Purpose.* Reread your opening paragraph or sentence (or second paragraph in the diamond sequence) to see if you have clearly stated the purpose of your letter. If your recipient had time to read only the first few lines of your message, would he or she understand why you are writing? Delete any unnecessary introductory material, wordy phrases, or background information if it obscures your point.

▶ *Focus on recipient.* Is your message recipient-based as well as writer-based? Have you taken the time to consider the recipient's characteristics and motivators? Make sure your tone and language level are appropriate.

▶ *Scope and meaning of topic.* What does your recipient really need to know about the topic? Have you included unnecessary information? Read through your letter to determine if you have discussed only what is relevant to your message.

▶ *Organization.* Good organization ensures the logical flow of ideas from one paragraph to another. Look over the various organizing formulas presented in the chapter to make sure you have chosen the best one for your letter.

   Read through your letter and mentally circle your main point. Except for the diamond sequence, if your main point comes in the second or third paragraph, your organization may be faulty. Revise your letter so the main point appears in the opening paragraph or immediately after the introductory material in the diamond sequence.

▶ *Closing.* Your closing should state clearly what you want the recipient to do or to remember. Don't assume your reader will guess or somehow ''know'' what is important or what action to take.

▶ *Language.* Have you adopted the right tone, eliminated wordy phrases and clichés, and used the active voice? Can you eliminate *there is* and *there are* from the beginning of your sentences and start out more forcefully? Can you condense clauses and phrases beginning with *which, who,* and *that* into fewer words?

   Reread your letter to see where you can streamline your language and use your own words to create vivid, effective communication.

▶ *Sentence length and structure.* Read your letter aloud, paying particular attention to the length and structure of your sentences. Do they average seventeen to twenty words? Have you varied their structure to mimic the tone and rhythms of natural speech?

Your sentences should draw attention to the *message,* not to themselves. If your sentences are too short or too long, overly complex or monotonous, they detract from your letter. Good sentence structure should lead the reader quickly and easily through your message.

▶ *Use of paragraphs, lists, and punctuation.* The main purpose of these devices is to highlight information and to make your letter easier to read. Remember to discuss only one idea per paragraph and keep paragraphs to within five to seven sentences. List information where appropriate. Keep the lists brief and use them selectively. Use capitalization, underscoring, and punctuation sparingly to highlight key information or ideas.

Look over the first version and revised version of the completed insurance letter:

Original

March 20, 19--   Policy #224-80-6H

Ms. Rhonda Graves
Mutual of St. Louis
45 East Victor Blvd.
St. Louis, MO 63142

Dear Rhonda:

I am making a career change in two months and must reduce my monthly expenses for a time. As a result, I would like to decrease my life insurance policy to $20,000 with a $50 monthly premium. Can you make the change by the first of the month?

Because both my parents are now deceased, I would like to change the beneficiary of my policy. Please fill in the names of my brother Charles Richmond and his wife Arlene Elizabeth as the new beneficiaries.

Let's keep the same automatic payment arrangement with the new policy as we had with the old. I believe all you have to do is tell the bank how much is to be deducted each month from my checking account. If you can, send me a schedule of premium increases for the next five years. That way, I'll know how much is being deducted each year for the premiums.

Will I be able to keep the same accident insurance rider? My accountant seemed to think it was a good addition to the policy. Let me know if I have to apply for it again with the new policy.

I'd like the new life insurance policy, complete with the changes discussed above, to take effect by the first of this month. If this is not possible, let me know and we can set a new date. Please send the new policy, along with a schedule of premium increases, to my current address. I appreciate your help in taking care of this matter.

Sincerely,

Allen Yankowitz

Allen Yankowitz
412 Morningside Lane
Wilmette, IL 60091

Revised

March 20, 19--   Policy #224-80-6H

Ms. Rhonda Graves
Mutual of St. Louis
45 East Victor Blvd.
St. Louis, MO 63142

Dear Rhonda:

I am making a career change in two months and must reduce my monthly expenses for a time. As a result, I would like to decrease my life insurance policy to $20,000 with a $50 monthly premium.

I would like you to make these and the following changes by the first of the month.

— Change the beneficiary from my parents (now deceased) to my brother Charles Richmond and his wife Arlene Elizabeth Yankowitz.

— Maintain the same automatic payment arrangement with my bank for the monthly premiums.

— Keep the same accident rider—let me know if I have to apply for it again with the new policy.

— Send me a schedule of premium increases over the next five years—I'll need this for my budget.

I'd like the new life insurance policy, complete with the changes above, to take effect by the first of this month. If this is not possible, let me know and we can set a new date.

Please send the new policy, along with a schedule of premium increases, to my current address. I really appreciate your help in taking care of this matter.

Sincerely,

Allen Yankowitz

Allen Yankowitz
412 Morningside Lane
Wilmette, IL 60091

In the revised version, the writer has used listing to highlight important information and make the letter easier to read.

Proofreading Your Letter

After going through the revision checklist, carefully proofread your final letter. If you have time, let someone else proofread it as well. The best way to proofread your letter is to go through it systematically.

First, check the format. Is the inside address or heading correct? Have you correctly placed the salutation, complimentary closing, and signature lines? Is the postscript, enclosures, or copies line clearly written?

Second, check names, dates, figures, times, and other facts for accuracy. This step is particularly important when you are sending out invitations or announcements.

Third, read through the letter for spelling errors and typographical mistakes. For example, have you used *there* for *their*? Have you transposed letters or omitted them from any words? Have you left out or repeated words in your sentences?

Finally, be sure to sign the letter before mailing it. Although this might sound like an obvious step, it is surprising how easily it can be overlooked.

The next chapter discusses in detail the different parts of formal and informal letters, letter formats for typing or writing your message, and essential mailing information.

CHAPTER
≡THREE

PRODUCING YOUR LETTERS

Now that you have worked on the content of your message, you are ready to put the letter in final form. Whether your message is formal or informal, you want to give your words a neat, attractive appearance. This not only makes your message easier to read but is a courtesy to the recipient.

This chapter reviews handwritten versus typed letters, letter formats, the correct forms for various parts of a letter, addressing envelopes, and basic mailing guidelines for domestic and foreign mail.

HANDWRITTEN VERSUS TYPED LETTERS

Many people want to know when it is appropriate to handwrite or type their letters. The general rule of thumb was to type all formal or business correspondence and handwrite most social correspondence to friends and family.

Today, however, the pace of many people's lives and the advent of personal computers have changed the old guidelines considerably. Many people do not have the time to sit down and handwrite their letters. As a result, it is now acceptable to type even social correspondence. As a courtesy to the reader, however, you might begin a typed social letter with a simple line such as, ''Please excuse the typewriter [or computer], but I wanted to make sure you heard from me.'' This gives a personal touch to the message.

Typewritten letters are still the best choice for formal or business correspondence. They are easier to read and give your message an official look.

However, in some instances, handwritten letters to public officials, politicians, and the media can grab more attention. Your letter's unspoken statement is that you took the time and effort to handwrite a personal message. As long as your handwriting is clear, you can put across your message with considerable impact. Many politicians report that they pay more attention to handwritten mail simply because it is not a form letter or mass mailing.

Circumstances and your lifestyle will determine whether you type or handwrite many of your letters. Even though typing may be more convenient, keep in mind that in social correspondence nothing can match the personal touch of a handwritten letter. It may be worth the extra effort.

FORMATS FOR LETTERS

Four basic formats are used in social and formal correspondence: full block, block, semiblock, and simplified (used only for formal letters). The full block format is easiest to use since all lines are flush with the left margin. Some people, however, prefer a more varied or balanced look to their letters and use the semiblock formats, in which the complimentary close and signature block appear near the center of the page.

Whichever format you choose, be consistent. Don't mix styles, using indented paragraphs with a flush left complimentary close and signature block. The appearance of your letter on the page can influence the reader's perception of your message. Figures 3.1 through 3.4 provide examples of full block, block, semiblock, and simplified formats.

Figure 3.1 Full Block

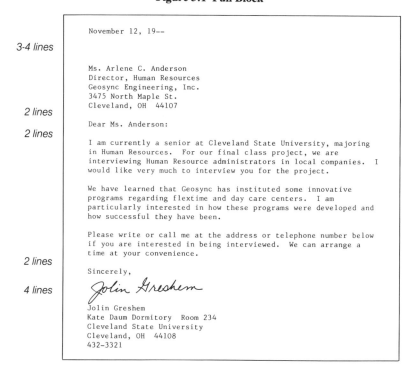

•All lines are set flush with the left margin.   •No paragraphs are indented.

Figure 3.2 Block

April 3, 19--

3-4 lines

Mr. Peter M. Anton
Station Manager
WREQ
1967 West Lawndale Dr.
Phoenix, AZ 85014

2 lines

Dear Mr. Anton:

2 lines

I don't often write about programs I hear on radio, but your broadcast Tuesday, April 1, was a new low in bad taste. I realize that April Fool's Day encourages practical jokes, but broadcasting that a truckload of poisonous snakes had overturned on the highway near our suburb was anything but funny.

My two children, already afraid of the rattlesnakes we get occasionally in our yard, heard the broadcast and were terrified. They refused to go out of the house and couldn't sleep for the next two nights.

Please, the next time you think up a practical joke, think again! Around here, poisonous snakes are no joke.

2 lines

Truly yours,

Linda S. Truckman

4 lines

(Mrs.) Linda S. Truckman

2 lines

cc: Georgia Nuessman, President

•Date line is flush with the right margin. •Heading or inside address, salutation, reference lines, and paragraphs set flush with the left margin. •Complimentary close and signature are aligned with the date.

Figure 3.3 Semiblock

	June 4, 19--
2 lines	
	481 Kimble Drive
	Fort Wayne, IN 46808
2 lines	
	Dear Katie,
2 lines	
	Excuse the typewriter but I've only got an hour before we have to leave on our trip. I wanted to get this letter off to you before we left.
	I agree that you can't change anyone or run their life, but I'm concerned about you more than about your sister. You haven't had a chance to pursue your own dreams--you've been too busy trying to help Linda. Let the hospital staff do that now. It's not your job to be her counselor or therapist.
	Please don't think I'm being hard on Linda. It's just that there has been no one there for you all these years. Why not start caring for Katie now?
2 lines	
	Love,
4 lines	*Pat*
2 lines	
	P.S. I'll write more when we get to Denver.

•Date is flush with the right margin.   •Heading or inside address and salutation are set flush with the left margin.   •Paragraphs are indented.   •Complimentary close and signature line are slightly to the right of the page's center.

Figure 3.4 Simplified

6 lines

February 14, 19--

4 lines

Edward C. Cooper, PhD
Director - Rsearch and Development
Fleeting Electronics Co.
5407 Collings Lane
Pittsburgh, PA 15234

3 lines

ULTRA SOUND ELECTRONICS CONFERENCE PROCEEDINGS

3 lines

The 15th Annual Ultra Sound Electronics Conference was one of the best ever. We had more exhibitors and presentors than in any other year.

The Conference Board is offering a bound volume of all papers presented at the conference during the four-day sessions. You can obtain a copy of this valuable resource for only $85.00 plus $4.00 handling and postage.

Please fill out the enclosed card and order your copy without delay. Once you've looked over the volume, we're sure you will agree this year's conference presented an outstanding offering of topics and speakers.

4-5 lines

JACKSON L. PARKER, PHD
CONFERENCE BOARD CHAIRMAN

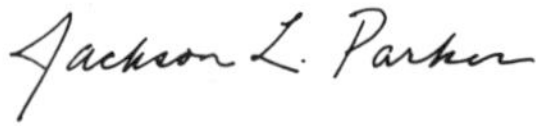

Jackson L. Parker

•No salutation or complimentary close.   •All lines begin flush with the left margin.   •Date is six lines below the letterhead.   •Inside address is four or more lines below the dateline.   •Subject line is typed in all caps, three lines below the inside address and above the body of the letter.
•Writer's name and title are typed in caps, four or five lines below the body of the letter.

STATIONERY

If you use personalized stationery for your correspondence, always write or type the first page of your letter on a letterhead page. If your letter runs two or more pages, use blank sheets that match the quality and color of the letterhead.

In formal correspondence, such as to a company or public official, repeat the recipient's name, the page number, and the date on all pages after the letterhead. Type this information six lines below the top of the page. The line can be typed either across the page or in block format, depending on how your letterhead is arranged on the page. The guiding rule is to give the letter a balanced look.

Mr. Ronald Talbot, 2   April 19, 19--

OR

Mr. Ronald Talbot
Page 2
April 19, 19--

If you are addressing more than one individual, arrange the names in alphabetical order:

Mr. Ronald Talbot   April 19, 19--
Ms. Carla Walker
Osgood Ford Dealership, 2

In social correspondence, date the first page and simply number the succeeding pages. You do not need to carry over your recipient's name or the date.

April 19, 19--

Dear Julia,

OR

Dear Julia,   April 19, 19--

INSIDE ADDRESS AND SALUTATION

The inside address and salutation are always typed flush with the left margin. In formal correspondence, the salutation is followed by a colon; in informal correspondence, it is followed by a comma.

Information in the inside address appears in the following order:

Individual's name and title
Company department or division (or agency, organization)
Company name (or government department)
Street address
City, state, and ZIP code

Salutation

Mrs. Geraldine Y. Sturgeon
Director, Public Relations
Office of the Mayor
453 N. Dearborn
Chicago, IL 60603

Mr. Duncan Isle
Vice President—Sales
Tri-State Shipping Co.
8421 South Holland Ave.
San Francisco, CA 94115

Dear Mrs. Sturgeon:

Dear Mr. Isle:

If you need to carry over a long line, indent the second line five spaces.

Ms. Patricia Stern
Director
American Association of Retired
    Physicians

Titles in the Inside Address

Various courtesy titles are used with people's names in formal and informal correspondence: Mr., Mrs., Miss, Ms., Dr., Professor, and the like. Chapter 4 presents correct forms of address and salutation for social occasions, and for various government, business, military, religious, and political individuals.

When addressing two or more people in a company, agency, institution or organization, use the following guidelines:

1. When addressing both men and women, list the names alphabetically or according to seniority in each rank.

> Ms. Kelley C. Vale, Director   *OR*   Mr. Raymond A. Heinz
> Mr. Raymond A. Heinz   Ms. Kelley C. Vale
>
> Dear Ms. Vale and Mr. Heinz: Dear Mr. Heinz and Ms. Vale:

2. When addressing two or more men in formal or business correspondence, use *Messrs.* (abbreviation of *Messieurs*, French for "misters").

> Mr. Raymond A. Heinz
> Mr. Huey R. Underwood
>
> Dear Messrs. Heinz and Underwood:

3. If you are addressing two or more women in formal or business correspondence, use *Mesdames, Mmes., Mlles.,* or *Mses.* Mlles. refers to younger or single women only.

> Ms. Ruby Lewis Day   Miss Arlene Nichols
> Mrs. Jennifer Stone   Miss Joan Banner
>
> Dear Mses. Day and Stone: Dear Mlles. Nichols and Banner:

4. When you don't know the gender of the person, or the name could be that of either a man or a woman, a new practice suggests using the single letter *M* as the courtesy title. Or you can simply use the full name in the salutation.

> M. Pat Justine   *OR*   Pat Justine
> Customer Relations   Customer Relations
> Springvale Office Supplies   Springvale Office Supplies
> (address)   (address)
>
> Dear M. Justine: Dear Pat Justine:

5. If you know only the department within a company but not a particular individual, put the company name first followed by the department name.

> Sears, Roebuck Co.
> Automotive Division
> 809 South Skokie Blvd.
> Skokie, IL 60076
>
> Dear Staff:

Street Addresses and P.O. Box Numbers

The following guidelines will help you address your correspondence both in the inside address and on the envelope.

1. Suite, room, or apartment numbers follow the street address on the same line, separated by a comma.

> 445 North Michigan, Room 812
> Chicago, IL 60611
>
> 17 West Superior, Apt. 19
> New York, NY 10017

2. If the inside address contains both a street address and a post office box, use the post office box, placing any postal station after the box number.

> P.O. Box 3425, Central Station   *OR*   P.O. Box 3425
> Central Station

If you must list both the post office box and street address, the post office will send the letter to whichever is directly above the city and state line. For faster delivery, put the P.O. number above the city and state or use the P.O. number alone. This is because the post office takes longer to route mail to a street address.

Customer Service
Hanover Assurance Co.
296 S. Crawford Ave.
P.O. Box 117
Omaha, Nebraska 68120

Customer Service
Hanover Assurance Co.
P.O. Box 117
Omaha, Nebraska 68120

3. The number *one* is always written out in an address. Numbered streets ten and below are written out, while street names over ten are typed as numbers.

One Washington Square
12 Fourth Avenue
183 - 23rd Street

Notice that a hyphen is inserted between building and street numbers to avoid confusion. Put a space on each side of the hyphen.

4. When compass directions come before a numbered street, use cardinal numbers (11, 12, 13 . . .).When they come after the street, use ordinal numbers (11th, 12th, 13th . . .).

459 West 65 Street   459 - 65th Street SE

Notice that no comma is placed between the street address and the compass abbreviation and no periods are used in the abbreviation.

Abbreviations.   For *formal correspondence*, spell out all words in an inside address, except for compass directions following the street name.

Wrong
42 Benson Blvd.
886 N. Holland Ave.
886 Holland Avenue,
  Northwest

Right
42 Benson Boulevard
886 North Holland Avenue
886 Holland Avenue NW

The post office prefers the two-letter abbreviation for states (for example, MN for Minnesota). However, you may want to spell out the state name in the inside address. Postal code abbreviations are included in the appendix.

Company abbreviations must follow the style preferred by each firm (Company, Co., Incorporated, Inc., Ltd., Associates, Assoc.). The complete company name can be found either on its stationery or by calling the firm.

Informal correspondence allows you to use abbreviations for street addresses, compass directions, and states.

338 N. Rockway Ave.	45 - 112th St. NE
Tampa, FL 33376	St. Petersburg, CA 93442

COMPLIMENTARY CLOSE

Formal and informal correspondence require different complimentary closes, but all of them are followed by a comma. The following lists will help you choose which closing is most appropriate for your letters.

Formal	*Less Formal*	*Informal*
Use in diplomatic or religious correspondence	Use for institutions, government agencies, prestigious associations, and companies	Use in general correspondence and with friends, family
Respectfully yours, Respectfully,	Very truly yours, Yours truly, Yours very truly, Very cordially yours, Very sincerely yours,	Sincerely, Sincerely yours, Best regards, Best wishes, Cordially, Cordially yours, Regards, Love, Kindest (warmest) regards,

SIGNATURE BLOCK

The signature block contains your name and, in formal correspondence, your title. The letter format you use dictates where on the page the signature block appears. In full block and simplified formats, the signature is flush with the left margin. In semiblock, it is slightly to the right of the center of the page. In block format, the signature block is flush with the right margin.

Informal Letters

The signature block for informal letters to friends and family generally contains only your first name or your first and last names. There is no need to type your name after the signature. Even if you type your letters, sign your name by hand.

Full Block or Simplified

Best regards,

Brian Swrina

Semiblock

Warmest Wishes,

Claudia Gold

Block

Kindest regards,

Randi Light

Formal Letters

Letters for more formal occasions or to businesses, politicians, government agencies, associations, and the like require a more formal signature block. Your name and title are typed four spaces below the complimentary close, leaving space for a signature.

Block

Sincerely yours,

Gordon H. Hasrow

Gordon H. Hasrow

Courtesy Titles. The only titles that precede a writer's name are *Mrs.*, *Miss*, or *Ms.* Their use is optional—usually to indicate that the writer is a woman if it is not clear from the name. These titles are enclosed in parentheses.

Semiblock
Very truly yours,

$Pat\ B.\ Peddleton$

(Mrs.) Pat B. Peddleton

Women can use a variety of titles, depending on their preference. Think about how you want your name to appear before you write it. Generally, divorced women who retain their ex-husband's last name do not use his first name in their signature block (for example: *Mrs. Fred Gowan* becomes *Mrs. Karen Gowan*). People will follow your lead and use the name as you have signed it in your letters.

Full Block
Sincerely yours,

(Mrs. Arthur T. Ritter)

Block
Truly yours,

(Ms.) Marika Graham

Titles Following a Name. If you are writing in an official capacity, you can include your job title either following your name or placed directly below it.

Full Block
Truly yours,

Jane O. Wilson, Director

Semiblock
Truly yours,

Jane O. Wilson
Director, Sales and Marketing

If you are writing for a company, the simplified format may be best. In this style, the company name or your name is typed in all capitals four lines below the end of the letter—there is no complimentary close. If the company name is used, your name is typed four lines below the company name. Otherwise, you sign your name below the all-capitals typed name.

Simplified	*Semiblock*
SKYLER, WARREN & ASSOCIATES	BRUCE C.NEULAND SENIOR PARTNER
Bruce C. Neuland	*Bruce C. Neuland*
Bruce C. Neuland Senior Partner	

Postscript

The postscript or P.S. line in a letter is typed two lines below the signature. In informal correspondence, the P.S. line comes after the signature but may be more or less than two lines down.

Full Block

Yours truly,

Dwayne P. Nolan

Dwayne P. Nolan

P.S. I just received your letter—it took 12 days to get here!

Signing for Someone Else

Occasionally you may have to act as secretary for someone and sign either that person's name or your own in place of his or hers. If you sign for someone else, place your initials on the same line and to the right of the signature.

Respectfully yours,

Sarah Chang   *J. J.*

(Mrs.) Sarah Chang

If you also composed the letter, sign your own name above the typed title "Secretary to . . . ."

Sincerely,

Shirley Heidt

Secretary to Morris Watson, Jr.

REFERENCE LINES

On occasion, you may need to use the reference lines *Attention, Personal, Confidential*, and other lines for special purposes.

Attention Line

The attention line is used to alert the person you are writing or to guarantee that your letter will be opened even if the recipient is absent. The attention line is typed two lines below the inside address and may be centered on the page or typed flush left. The word "Attention" is used with an initial capital only and followed by a colon. When possible, use the recipient's full name.

Attention: Ms. Carla E. Wainright

Personal and Confidential

A personal or confidential notation indicates that only the recipient should open the letter. Type *Personal* or *Confidential* four lines above the inside address and underscore it. Use this reference line only for matters that are strictly personal.

Personal

Mrs. Bernice R. Simpson
Assistant Director, Volunteers
St. Joseph's Hospital
4545 East Riverside
New York, NY 10021

Other Reference Lines

In some instances you may have to cite document numbers, serial or model numbers, your credit card or account number, or a letter you wrote previously in your current message. Type the information about four lines below the date, flush with the right margin, and on the same line as the first line of the inside address.

August 19, 19--

Mastercard   Account No. 3462-34623-1221
South Chemical Bank
P.O. Box 211
Terre Haute, IN 47815

ADDRESSING THE ENVELOPE

The final step in producing your letter is addressing the envelope. You don't want to jeopardize your message by careless mistakes in the street address or ZIP code. The U.S. Postal Service provides guidelines for streamlining your mail and ensuring fast delivery in their publications. You can obtain copies from your local post office or by writing to Marketing & Communications, U.S. Postal Service, P.O. Box 31621, Louisville, KY 40231-9621.

The address area read by the postal equipment is an imaginary space on the envelope five-eighths inch from the bottom with one-inch margins on the right and left sides of the address. All non-address information, such as company logo and personalized initials or other designs, should be above the city, state, and ZIP code line, as shown in Figure 3.5.

Figure 3.5 Address Area on Envelope

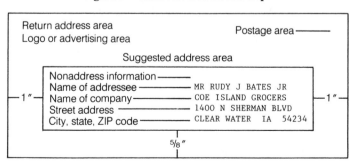

Informal Letters

When addressing informal correspondence to family and friends, use the following order of information on the envelope.

Name (including any titles)
Street address and suite or apartment number
City and state plus ZIP code
Country (if other than United States)

This information is placed somewhat to the right of the center of the envelope. Make sure all figures are clearly legible.

Your return address is always placed in the upper left-hand corner of the envelope. It should include your last name; street address; city, state, and ZIP code; and "U.S.A." if the letter is addressed to a foreign country.

The U.S. Postal Service has clear guidelines for addressing envelopes that will help speed your mail through the automatic sorting system. These guidelines apply to informal letters as well as business and more formal correspondence. The preferred style is illustrated in Figure 3.6.

According to U.S. Postal guidelines the address should:

1. Be machine printed or typewritten.

2. Be written in all capital letters.

3. Be double-spaced between lines.

4. Be without punctuation (periods or commas). Use one or two spaces between words instead of punctuation.

5. Include floor, suite, apartment, condominium number, and directionals (North, East, and so forth). The recommended abbreviations for these elements are contained in the Appendix to this book.

6. Use the two-letter abbreviation for states, territories, and other countries. State, territory, and country abbreviations are provided in the Appendix.

Figure 3.6 U.S. Postal Service Style for Envelopes

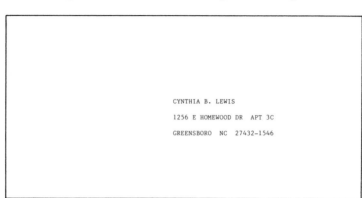

CYNTHIA B. LEWIS

1256 E HOMEWOOD DR   APT 3C

GREENSBORO   NC   27432-1546

7. Use the ZIP code appropriate for the city and state in the U.S., and the postal code for foreign countries for letters sent abroad.

The ZIP + 4 Code adds four additional numbers to the five-digit ZIP Codes to enable automated equipment to sort mail more quickly and efficiently. To date, however, only businesses and other professional institutions regularly use the additional four-digit number.

Postal codes for foreign countries can be obtained from your local post office.

8. Be typed in black or printed in dark ink on light-colored paper. Avoid using italic or exotic typefaces or having the letters touch each other—the automated machinery has trouble reading such characters.

9. Be parallel to the bottom of the envelope. Make sure the lines are straight, not skewed or slanted.

Envelopes for informal correspondence can be typed or handwritten, as shown in Figure 3.7. Handwritten addresses should follow the above guidelines as closely as possible.

Figure 3.7 Sample Envelopes

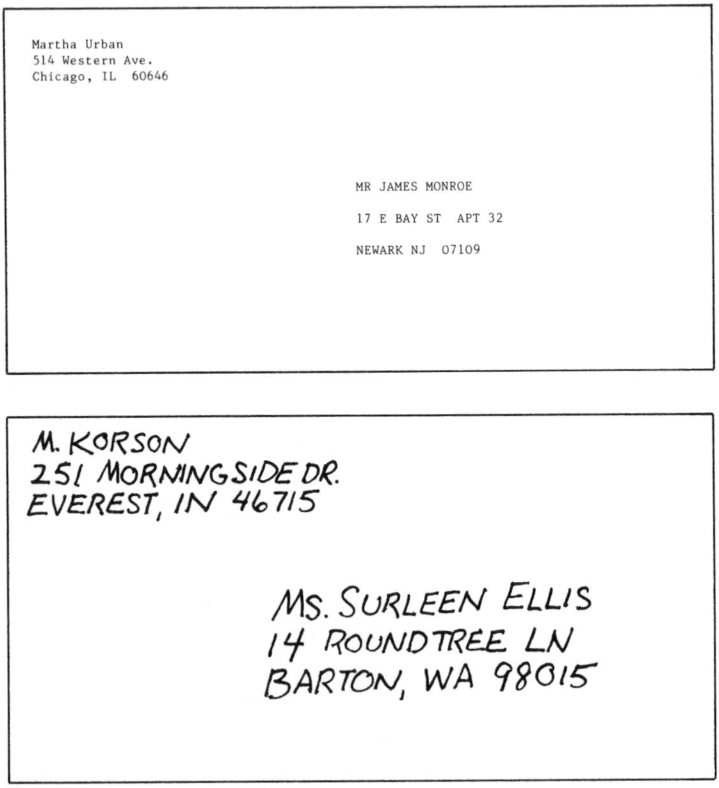

```
Martha Urban
514 Western Ave.
Chicago, IL  60646




                              MR  JAMES  MONROE

                              17  E  BAY  ST    APT  32

                              NEWARK  NJ    07109
```

```
M. KORSON
251 MORNINGSIDE DR.
EVEREST, IN 46715


              MS. SURLEEN ELLIS
              14 ROUNDTREE LN
              BARTON, WA 98015
```

Formal Letters

Envelopes for formal letters include more information, given in the following order:

Name of the individual or the company, agency, institution
Title of individual
Department or division
Company, agency, institution name
Street address plus suite, room, floor numbers
Post office box number
City, state, and ZIP code
Country (if sent abroad)

You may not have enough room on your envelope to double space all this information. In that case, single space the address, using the guidelines above.

MS MARIE DEPLEISS
DIRECTOR MARKETING
ANTOINE PRINTERS INC
14 N OHIO SUITE 503
P O BOX 45672
FRENCH LICK IN 47432-8734

For formal correspondence, the Postal Service recommends that you maintain at least a one-inch margin on the right-hand side of the address and at least a half-inch margin on the bottom.

The guidelines for special notations on your formal correspondence are as follows:

1. Type special mailing instructions (SPECIAL DELIVERY, EX-PRESS MAIL, PRIORITY MAIL) in all capitals two lines below the area where the stamps are placed.

2. Type the attention line above the company name.

ATTN JONATHAN HODGES
JOHNSON & KEIL INC
14 N 41ST ST
BARKLEY UT 84713-8623

3. Type the personal or confidential line two lines above and just to the left of the address.

Confidential

DR ZUHIN BHOTA
OBSTETRICS AND GYNECOLOGY RM 34
LAWRENCE MEDICAL CENTER
1534 WADE AVE NE
KANSAS CITY MO 64112-1245

MAILING GUIDELINES

Postal rates and instructions are changing all the time—for the latest information, call your local post office. However, keep these few guidelines in mind when mailing your letters.

U.S. Mail

Most of your correspondence will go first class. Because nearly all interstate mail and most intrastate mail is delivered by air, domestic airmail rates have been virtually eliminated for first-class mail. However, you do have a few choices when your letter needs to be delivered overnight, when you need verification that a letter or document reached its destination, or when you are doing a bulk mailing for your club, volunteer organization, or association.

1. *Express Mail*—This service guarantees overnight delivery to all cities receiving the service. It is quite expensive, however.

2. *Registered or Certified Letter*—This service guarantees you will receive written notification that the letter or document was delivered. Whoever receives the letter must sign for it. The receipt is then mailed back to you with the date of delivery written on it.

3. *Bulk mailings*—The post office provides reduced rates for bulk mailings of two hundred or more, if you qualify for the service. Check with your local post office regarding procedures to apply for a bulk mailing number.

4. *Second-class mail*—This service covers postcards and letters that are not sealed. Although the rate is cheaper, your messages are not as secure.

Foreign Mail

Foreign mail can be delivered either airmail or surface mail by ship. The delivery times and postal rates can be dramatically different. In some instances, a letter can take ten days by air and six to eight weeks by ship to reach its intended receiver. Find out from your post office what types of services are available to the country your message is meant to reach.

Postal rates are based not only on weight but on geographic region. For example, Canadian rates are the same as those in the United States. Mailing a letter to any Canadian city is like mailing a letter from one U.S. city to another. Postal rates for letters going to European nations are roughly the same for all Western European states, whether your letter is going to England, West Germany, France, or Spain. Rates to South America, Africa, Asia, and Australia differ depending on the country and what type of service you select.

Always consult your local post office for the latest mailing information.

CHAPTER
≡Four

How to Address
Just About Anyone

At one time or another you will need to write a senator or representative, a religious leader, a company official, or other professional or civic officials. Many people put off writing such letters because they don't know how to address the recipient. What is the correct title for a Protestant minister? How do you address your congressperson? Do you address a divorced woman by her former husband's last name or by her maiden name?

Knowing the proper form of address is not only good etiquette, it can also help to ensure that the recipient takes your letter seriously. This chapter shows you how to address many of the individuals you may have occasion to write. The reference section of the public library is an excellent source for forms of address not listed in this chapter.

SOCIAL TITLES
Men

Use the title *Mr.* unless the man has a professional title such as *Dr.*, *Professor, President,* or other.

Mr. Walter C. Paton	*OR*	Dr. Walter C. Paton
763 Burton Drive		Alaster Corporation
Ryker, OH 45775		Market Research
		213 Fifth Avenue
Dear Mr. Paton,		Nashville, AL 35578
		Dear Dr. Paton:

In the United States, it is customary to use only one title with the name, although other countries often use more than one. Look over the examples of incorrect and correct usage. The title *Esquire* or *Esq.* may be used when addressing a lawyer or diplomatic consul.

Incorrect		*Correct*
Dr. Edward P. Planton, MD		Dr. Edward P. Planton *OR*
		Edward P. Planton, MD
Honorable Arthur C. Chavez, Esq.		Arthur C. Chavez, Esq.
Dr. Phillip D. Pierre	*OR*	Phillip D. Pierre, PhD

When a man has *Jr.* or *Sr.* or a roman numeral after his last name, do not repeat the abbreviation or numeral in the salutation.

Gregory W. Aton, Jr.	Dear Mr. Aton,
Thomas Edward Lawrence III	Dear Mr. Lawrence:

When you are addressing more than one man in the same letter, use *Mr.* before each name. In the salutation, *Mr.* is used with only the individuals' last names. (The French title *Messrs.* ["misters"] is used only in very formal or legal correspondence.)

Mr. Frank Costello
Mr. Thomas B. Hanover
Mr. Albert Wisenstein

Dear Mr. Costello, Mr. Hanover, and Mr. Wisenstein:

Women

The guidelines for addressing women are more complex, because several titles have developed over the centuries. Women have been addressed as *Miss, Mrs., Ms., Madame (Mme.), Mademoiselle (Mlle.),* or *Mesdames (Mses.).* The only rule regarding the correct form of address is to follow what the woman herself prefers. If you don't know her preference, the following guidelines can help you to establish a style in your correspondence.

1. If marital status is unknown, use *Ms.*, unless the woman has a professional title (*Dr., Professor, President*).

Ms. Anita Yung	Dr. Anita Yung
Dear Ms. Yung,	Dear Dr. Yung:

2. Use *Miss* in formal correspondence if the woman is single and chooses not to use *Ms.*

   Miss Trisha North   Dear Miss North:

3. Use *Miss, Ms., Mrs.* before each woman's name when addressing more than one woman in the same letter. The social titles are used with the women's last names only in the salutation. The French titles *Mademoiselle (Mlle.)* and *Mesdames (Mmes.)* are used only in very formal circumstances, such as diplomatic or legal correspondence.

   Miss Anita Yung
   Mrs. Trisha North

   Dear Miss Yung and Mrs. North:

4. For most correspondence, use a married woman's first name, not her husband's. If she prefers a hyphenated maiden-married name, follow her style.

Ms. Lennea Robertson   Ms. Lennea Toll-Robertson

However, in formal social correspondence, it is customary to use the husband's first and last name when addressing the wife.

Mrs. Paul Robertson

5. If your reader is widowed or divorced, use her first and married name unless she has chosen to return to her maiden name. The title *Mrs.* is generally used if a woman has chosen to keep her married last name. However, if the woman prefers *Ms.* or has a professional title, use these titles.

Married	*Widowed or Divorced*
Mrs. Helene Farkas	Ms. Helene Huston
Mrs. Helene Huston-Farkas	Dr. Helene Farkas *OR*
	Dr. Helene Huston-Farkas

Married Couples

How to address married couples can be confusing these days. While few hard-and-fast rules exist, customary forms of address have been adjusted to the times.

1. The traditional form of address lists the husband and wife under the husband's last name.

Mr. and Mrs. Carlos R. Mendotta
OR
Mr. Carlos R. and Mrs. Pilar C. Mendotta

Dear Mr. and Mrs. Mendotta:

2. In many instances today, however, the couple's last name may include the wife's maiden name, or the wife may keep her maiden name, even though she is married. The forms of address for such couples are the following:

> Mr. and Mrs. Staton-Davis
> > *OR*
> Mr. and Mrs. Paul Staton-Davis
>
> Dear Mr. and Mrs. Staton-Davis:
>
> Mr. and Mrs. Paul Staton-Davis
> > *OR*
> Mr. Paul Davis and Ms. Susan Staton
>
> Dear Mr. Davis and Ms. Staton:

On the envelope, the two names are stacked one over the other. Although the husband's name is traditionally listed first, some people prefer to list them alphabetically to avoid the issue of whether the man or woman comes first.

> Mr. Angelo Withers   *OR*   Ms. Harriet Appleton
> Ms. Harriet Appleton   Mr. Angelo Withers

3. When only the husband has a title, the customary form of address is as follows:

> Dr. and Mrs. Otto Wierner   Dear Dr. and Mrs. Wierner:
> > *OR*
> Judge and Mrs. Otto   Dear Judge and Mrs.
> Wierner   Wierner:

4. When only the wife has a title, the customary form of address is as follows:

> Dr. Julia and Mr. Otto   Dear Dr. and Mr. Wierner:
> Wierner
> > *OR*

Dr. Julia Wierner and   Dear Dr. and Mr. Wierner:
Mr. Otto Wierner

5. When both husband and wife have titles, any of the following forms is acceptable:

Drs. Barbara F. and Norman B. Custer
Dr. Barbara F. and Dr. Norman B. Custer
Drs. Norman B. and Barbara F. Custer
Dr. Norman B. and Dr. Barbara F. Custer

Dear Drs. Custer:

Gender Unknown

When the gender of the person you are addressing is not known and the name could be that of either a man or a woman, modern correspondence practice allows the use of the single letter *M.* as the title.

M. Pat Queenland   Dear M. Queenland:

If you need to write to a company, organization, or agency and do not have the name of an individual or know the gender of the staff, use one of the following forms of address:

Dear Sir or Madam:
To Whom It May Concern:
Dear (agency, department, or company) Manager:
Dear (agency, department, or company) Staff:

Always try to determine whether you are writing to a man or woman in your correspondence. If that is not possible, use the gender-inclusive forms above. Don't assume that the person receiving your letter will be a man or woman simply because of the company or agency you are writing.

COMPANY OFFICIALS

Titles in business have their own hierarchy. For most companies and corporations, the hierarchy moves from the chairperson of the board down to the line managers and supervisors. The possible list of titles is as follows:

Chairperson of the Board
President *OR* President and Chief Executive Officer
Executive Vice President
Associate Vice President
Vice President
Officer of the Corporation (Comptroller, Corporate Secretary, Treasurer)
Manager *OR* Director
Supervisor *OR* Superintendent

Your correspondence is likely to involve someone in middle or upper management or an officer of the company. Such titles are always included in the inside address but are not used in the salutation. The title may follow the individual's name or be listed underneath the name.

Timothy W. Kendall, Director *OR* Timothy W. Kendall
Marketing   Director, Marketing
Montgomery Ward   Montgomery Ward
4300 Rindal Drive   4300 Rindal Drive
Orlando, FL 32809   Orlando, FL 32809

Dear Mr. Kendall: Dear Mr. Kendall:

Try to find out the recipient's title before you write the letter. Your attention to such details can help to catch the recipient's eye and ensure that you are sending your letter to the right person.

If you don't know your recipient's name, use one of the gender-inclusive forms of address to avoid offending that person.

Marketing Department
Montgomery Ward
4300 Rindal Drive
Orlando, FL 32809

Dear Marketing Manager:
Dear Marketing Staff:
Dear Marketing Director:
Dear Sir or Madam:

STATE AND LOCAL GOVERNMENT

You will probably write state and local officials more than any other politicians. Look over the forms of address for government officials on the state and local level. Be sure to choose the appropriate formal title, such as *Sir* or *Madam*. The informal title generally includes the person's office (Mayor, District Attorney, and so on). Your public library can supply you with the address for any state or local official.

Governor, Acting Governor, Lieutenant Governor of State or Territory

Although most states use the form of address given below, the courtesy title in some states (and by law in Massachusetts) is *His/Her Excellency, the Governor of (State)*.

The Honorable Theodore R. Washington
Governor of Colorado

Dear Governor Washington:

The Honorable Judith E. Hupman
Acting Governor of New Mexico

Dear Ms. Hupman:

The Honorable Samuel F. Quinonas
Lieutenant Governor of Florida

Dear Mr. Quinonas:

Secretary of State

The Honorable Freida N. Yates
Secretary of the State of New Hampshire

Dear Ms. Secretary:

Attorney General

The Honorable Bernard O. Pulaski
Attorney General of Illinois

Dear Mr. Attorney General:

State Senate

President of Senate

The Honorable Irene G. Esterhaus
President of the Senate of the State of Ohio

Dear Ms. Esterhaus:

State Senators

The Honorable L. Richmond Peters
The State Senate

Dear Senator Peters:

State House of Representatives or Assembly

Different states call this body by different names. In New York, Wisconsin, Nevada, and California, it is called the Assembly. Maryland, West Virginia, and Virginia label theirs the House of Delegates, while in New Jersey it is known as the House of General Assembly.

Speaker of House or Assembly

The Honorable Gregory C. Delvecchio
Speaker of the Assembly of the State of Indiana

Dear Mr. Delvecchio:

State Representative, Assemblyman/woman, Delegate
The Honorable Evelyn C. Wong
House of Delegates (or House of Representatives or Assembly)

Dear Ms. Wong:

State Treasurer, Auditor, Comptroller
The Honorable Wilbur A. Stawinski
Treasurer (or Auditor or Comptroller) of the State of Maine

Dear Mr. Stawinski:

District Attorney
The Honorable Ophelia R. Hampstead
District Attorney, Welber County

Dear Ms. Hampstead:

City Officials
Mayor of a City or Town
The Honorable Vernon U. Nightwood
Mayor of Bensonville

Dear Mr. Mayor: *OR* Dear Mayor Nightwood:

President of Board of Commissioners
The Honorable Ruth D. Garson
President
Board of Commissioners of the City of Austin

Dear Ms. Garson:

Attorney, Counsel, Corporation Counsel
The Honorable Frank K. Constantine
City Attorney (or Counsel or Corporation Counsel)

Dear Mr. Constantine:

Alderman/woman and Committeeman/woman

Alderwoman Yolanda R. Ruiz-Mendosa
City Hall

Dear Ms. Ruiz-Mendosa:

COURT OFFICIALS

The U.S. judicial branch of government begins with the U.S. Supreme Court at the federal level and the state supreme courts at the local level. The federal court system includes a network of district and appellate courts. State judicial systems include state district and appellate courts along with local county courts.

U. S. Supreme Court

Chief Justice

The Chief Justice of the United States
The Supreme Court of the United States

Dear Mr. Chief Justice:

Associate Justice

Madam Justice O'Connor
The Supreme Court of the United States

Dear Madam Justice: *OR*   Dear Justice O'Connor:

State Supreme Court

Chief Justice, Chief Judge

The Honorable William B. Sasaki
Chief Justice of the Supreme Court of California

Dear Mr. Chief Justice:

Associate Justice

The Honorable Suzanne P. D'Orleans
Associate Justice of the Supreme Court of Louisiana

Dear Justice: *OR* Dear Justice D'Orleans:

Presiding Justice

The Honorable Howard M. Lebron
Presiding Judge, Appellate Division
Supreme Court of California

Dear Justice: *OR* Dear Justice Lebron:

Judge of a State or Federal Court (Other Than U. S. Supreme Court)

The Honorable Jennifer V. Riddley
Judge of the United States District Court for the
     Southern District of Utah (or other court name)

Dear Judge Riddley:

Clerk of a State or Federal Court

If you use the title *Esq. (Esquire)* with the name, drop the social titles *Mr., Mrs., Miss, Ms.*

Charles J. Chiang, Esq.
Clerk of the Superior Court of Iowa

Dear Mr. Chiang:

U. S. GOVERNMENT

This section includes the executive and legislative branches of the government. The judicial branch (Supreme Court and federal courts) is covered in the ''Court Officials'' section above. If the individual has a professional title, such as *Dr.*, substitute it for the social titles *Mr., Mrs., Miss, Ms.*

President and Former President

The President (or President George Bush or President Bush)
The White House

Dear Mr. President:

The Honorable Gerald R. Ford

Dear Mr. Ford:

Vice President/President of the Senate

Under the U.S. Constitution, the vice-president of the United States also serves as the president of the Senate.

The Vice-President of the United States (or Vice-President
    Quayle)
The White House

Dear Mr. Vice-President:

The Honorable J. Danforth Quayle
President of the Senate

Dear Mr. President: *OR* Dear Mr. Quayle:

House of Representatives

Speaker of the House.   The Speaker of the House is next in line for the presidency after the vice-president and secretary of state.

The Honorable Thomas S. Foley
Speaker of the House of Representatives

Dear Mr. Speaker: *OR* Dear Mr. Foley:

U.S. Representative or Congressman/woman
The Honorable Michael C. Korson
House of Representatives
(Washington, D.C. address)

(When away from Washington, D.C.)

The Honorable Michael C. Korson
Representative to Congress
(local address)

Dear Mr. Korson: *OR* Dear Representative Korson:

Senate

U.S. Senator
The Honorable Ruth O. Steinmetz
United States Senate

Dear Senator Steinmetz:

Committee/Subcommittee Chairs of Senate and House
The Honorable Lillian B. Kincaid
Chair
House Ways and Means Committee
House of Representatives

Dear Madam Chairwoman: *OR* Dear Representative Kincaid:

Cabinet Officers

The U.S. cabinet is composed of 14 offices, each with its own Secretary and Under Secretary (with the exception of the Attorney General). The cabinet departments are as follows: Agriculture, Attorney General, Commerce, Defense, Education, Energy, Health and Human Services, Housing and Urban Development, Interior, Labor, State, Transportation, Treasury, and Veterans' Affairs.

The Honorable James A. Baker III
Secretary of State

(Writing to a secretary from abroad)
The Honorable James A. Baker III
Secretary of State of the United States of America

Dear Mr. Baker: *OR* Dear Secretary Baker:

Under Secretary of a Department
The Honorable Glenda K. Yusef
Under Secretary of Labor

Dear Ms. Yusef: *OR* Dear Madam Under Secretary:

Attorney General
The Honorable Richard Thornburgh
Attorney General of the United States

Dear Mr. Thornburgh: *OR* Dear Attorney General:

Territorial Delegate or Resident Commissioner
The Honorable Jorge L. Charro
Delegate of Puerto Rico
House of Representatives

Dear Mr. Charro:

The Honorable Morton S. Turpin
Resident Commissioner of (Territory)
House of Representatives

Dear Mr. Turpin:

Heads of Agencies, Organizations, Commissions

The Honorable Lucy S. Moy
Atomic Energy Commission (or agency or organization name)

Dear Ms. Moy: *OR* Dear Madam Director:

Other High Officials

The Honorable Carl F. Hansen
Superintendent of Documents (or other official title)

Dear Mr. Hansen:

U.S. DIPLOMATIC REPRESENTATIVES

The diplomatic corps represents our nation abroad in various countries. Ambassadors and ministers to Central or South American nations substitute *The Ambassador of the United States* for the title *American Ambassador* or *American Minister*.

If the diplomat holds military rank, substitute the rank for the complimentary title *The Honorable* (for example, *Colonel* William S. Duncan, *American Ambassador*).

When the diplomat is not at his or her post, add the name of the country in which the individual is based: (Colonel William S. Duncan, *American Ambassador to Ireland*).

Ambassador

The Honorable Kristen G. Mandala
American Ambassador

Dear Ambassador: *OR* Dear Ambassador Mandala:

Minister

The Honorable Jeffry S. Larson III
American Minister to Zaire

Dear Mr. Minister: *OR* Dear Minister Larson:

Chargé d'Affaires, Consul General, Consul, Vice Consul

Vivian B. Jordan, Esq.
American Chargé d'Affaires (or Consul General, Consul, Vice
    Consul)

Dear Ms. Jordan:

High Commissioner

The Honorable Thomas R.R. Quincy
United States High Commissioner to Peru

Dear Mr. Quincy:

FOREIGN DIPLOMATIC REPRESENTATIVES

The correct form of address for most foreign diplomats is given below. However, British representatives are addressed as *British Ambassador* or *British Minister*. Use the form of address *The Right Honorable* or *The Honorable* in addition to *His/Her Excellency* wherever appropriate when writing to the British representative or a member of the British Commonwealth. If the diplomat has a royal title, *His/Her Excellency* or *The Honorable* would be omitted.

Ambassador to the United States

His Excellency Karl Otto Zufle
Ambassador of Germany

Formal
Excellency:

Informal
Dear Mr. Ambassador:

Foreign Minister to the United States

The Honorable Njoki Nalumwa
Minister of Kenya

Formal	*Informal*
Madam:	Dear Madam Minister:

His Highness Anjou de la Roche
Minister of Monte Carlo

Formal	*Informal*
Sir:	Dear Minister de la Roche:

Prime Minister

His Excellency, Steingrimur Hermannsson
Prime Minister of the Republic of Iceland

Formal	*Informal*
Excellency:	Dear Mr. Prime Minister:

British Prime Minister

The Right Honorable John Major
Prime Minister

Formal	*Informal*
Sir:	Dear Mr. Prime Minister: *OR*
	Dear Mr. Major:

Canadian Prime Minister

The Right Honorable Brian Mulroney
Prime Minister of Canada

Formal	*Informal*
Sir:	Dear Prime Minister: *OR*
	Dear Mr. Mulroney:

President of a Republic

His Excellency, Emmanuel Herarras
President of Panama

Formal	*Informal*
Excellency:	Dear Mr. President:

Premier

His Excellency, Vincente Gregorio
Premier of Italy

Formal	*Informal*
Excellency:	Dear Mr. Premier:

Chargé d'Affaires in the United States

Mr. Lars Jorgenssen
Chargé d'Affaires of Norway

Formal	*Informal*
Sir:	Dear Mr. Jorgenssen:

RELIGIOUS ORDERS

The forms of address given below should be used when writing any clergy of the Roman Catholic, Prostestant, or Jewish faiths. Buddhism, Islam, and Hinduism do not have formal clergy but do have religious scholars who serve within each faith.

Roman Catholic Church

The Pope

His Holiness, The Pope OR His Holiness, Pope John Paul
Vatican City

Your Holiness: OR Most Holy Father:

Cardinal

His Eminence, Paul Cardinal Taylor
Archbishop of Chicago

Formal	*Informal*
Your Eminence:	Dear Cardinal Taylor:

Bishop and Archbishop

The Most Reverend Paul Taylor, DD
Bishop (or Archbishop) of New Orleans

Formal	*Informal*
Your Excellency:	Dear Bishop: *OR*
	Dear Archbishop:

Monsignor

Reverend Msgr. Whitely S. Parke

Formal	*Informal*
Reverend Monsignor:	Dear Monsignor Tyler:

Priest

The Reverend Alfred I. Ingersoll

Dear Father Ingersoll:

Nun. Some women religious prefer to be addressed by their last name (Sister Anderson) rather than their first or given names (Sister Pauline). Use the form of address preferred by the woman if you know it.

Sister Pauline Anderson

Dear Sister: *OR* Dear Sister Pauline:

Protestant Churches

Archbishop

The Most Reverend Archbishop of Canterbury

OR

The Most Reverend Harold St. John
Archbishop of Canterbury

Formal	*Informal*
Your Grace:	Dear Archbishop St. John:

Bishop

The Right Reverend Louise Martinson
Bishop of Santa Fe

OR

The Reverend Louisa Martinson
Methodist Bishop

Formal	*Informal*
Right Reverend Madam: *OR* Reverend Madam:	Dear Bishop Martinson:

Archdeacon

The Venerable Richard Phillips
Archdeacon of San Francisco

Formal	*Informal*
Venerable Sir:	Dear Archdeacon:

Dean (Head of Cathedral or Theological Seminary)

The Very Reverend Warren C. Farrell
Dean of Garrett Seminary

Formal	*Informal*
Very Reverend Sir:	Dear Dean Farrell:

Priest or Minister

The Reverend Carol Y. Maddox

Dear Reverend Maddox:

Jewish Faith

Rabbi

Rabbi Frank C. Bernstein
OR
Rabbi Frank C. Bernstein, PhD (with academic degree)

Dear Rabbi Bernstein:
OR
Dear Dr. Bernstein: (with academic degree)

Buddhism, Islam, and Hinduism

Although these three faiths have no organized clergy, religious scholars are recognized as interpreters of scripture and leaders of individual religious communities. If you wish to know the correct title or form of address for an individual in one of these faiths, it is best to contact a temple or mosque in your area and speak with the head of the organization.

Buddhism.   Although most forms of Buddhism have no formal religious hierarchy, Tibetan Buddhism is an exception to the general rule. This branch of Buddhism is headed by a Dalai Lama, who is addressed as *His Holiness.*

Other Buddist monks, nuns, and priests may be addressed by honorary titles, such as *rinpoche.* When writing to Buddhist scholars other than the Dalai Lama, simply address them by their full name and honorary title, if any is given.

Chan Trang Rinpoche

Islam.   The head of a mosque is referred to as an *Imam*, while religious teachers and scholars are given the honorary title of *mullah*. In Iran, a leader of the faithful is known as an *ayatollah*. Use the honorary title and full name of the person to whom you are writing.

> Imam Ali Akbar Hussein

Hinduism.   Hinduism has several honorary titles given to those who are recognized as spiritually developed individuals. The title *Mahatma* (''great soul'') has been given to only a few people, such as the Hindu political and religious leader Gandhi. *Guru* (''spiritual guide'') is applied to someone who instructs students in spiritual disciplines. If you wish to write to these individuals, use their full name and honorary title, if it is known.

> Guru Rama Shastri

COLLEGE AND UNIVERSITY OFFICIALS
President

> Dr. Rosalind F. Karoll (with doctor's degree)
> President
> Northern University

> Dear Dr. Karoll:

> Ms. Rosalind F. Karoll (without doctor's degree)
> President
> Northern University

> Dear President Karoll:

Chancellor

Dr. Helen P. Garcia
Chancellor
Southwestern State University

Dear Dr. Garcia

Dean/Assistant Dean

Dr. Loretta G. Toland (with doctor's degree)
Dean, School of Business Administration
University of South Carolina

Dear Dean Toland: *OR* Dear Dr. Toland:

Assistant Dean Andrew Long (without doctor's degree)
School of Journalism
University of South Carolina

Dear Dean Long:

Professor

Full or Tenured Professor

Dr. Jill G. Schroeder *OR* Jill G. Schroeder, PhD
Eastern University

Dear Dr. Schroeder: *OR* Dear Professor Schroeder:

Associate, Assistant Professor

Dr. Henry Van Dyne *OR* Henry Van Dyne, PhD
Associate Professor
Iowa State University

Dear Dr. Van Dyne: *OR* Dear Professor Van Dyne:

Instructor

Dr. Linda S. Fraser *OR* Linda S. Fraser, PhD
Department of English
University of North Carolina

Dear Dr. Fraser:

Chaplain

Chaplain Carl B. Whitehead, DD, PhD
St. Andrew's College

Dear Dr. Whitehead:

The Reverend Barbara V. Browne
Chaplain
Northern College

Dear Chaplain Browne:

MILITARY OFFICIALS

When writing to someone in the military, include the person's full rank in the inside address and on the envelope but not in the salutation. In the Army, regular service is indicated by adding *USA* after the person's name, and the reserve is indicated by adding *USAR*. The formal title in the salutation for all military personnel is *Sir* or *Madam*.

Army, Air Force, Marine Corps

Army, Air Force, and Marine titles are the same, except that the top rank in the Marines is *Commandant of the Marine Corps*. Regular service in the Air Force and Marines is indicated by *USAF* and *USMC*, the reserve by *USAFR* and *USMCR*.

General of the Army or Air Force, Commandant of the Marine Corps

General of the Army Trenton G. Joslin, USA
Department of the Army

Dear General Joslin:

General of the Air Force Michael K. Eaton, USAF
Department of the Air Force

Dear General Eaton:

Commandant of the Marine Corps Chester S. Wylie, USMC
Marine Corps

Dear Commandant Wylie:

General, Lieutenant General, Major General, Brigadier General

Major General (or other rank) Vera T. Walker, USA

Dear General Walker:

Colonel, Lieutenant Colonel

Colonel (or Lieutenant Colonel) Daniel W. Quaid, USAF

Dear Colonel Quaid:

Major

Major Caroline N. Lewis, USA

Dear Major Lewis:

Captain

Captain Henry B. Kohl, USMC

Dear Captain Kohl:

First Lieutenant, Second Lieutenant

Lieutenant Ruth Y. DeBeere, USA

Dear Lieutenant DeBeere:

Chief Warrant Officer, Warrant Officer

Chief Warrant Officer George M. Pike, USAF

Dear Mr. Pike:

Chaplain

Chaplain Mark Petrakis, USA

Dear Chaplain Petrakis:

Navy, Coast Guard

Titles in the Navy and Coast Guard are the same, except that the top rank in the Navy is *Admiral*. Regular service is indicated by *USN* for the Navy and *USCG* for the Coast Guard. Reserve service is indicated by *USNR* and *USCGR*.

Fleet Admiral

Admiral Anhaus Rhinehart, USN
Chief of Naval Operations
Department of the Navy

Dear Admiral Rhinehart:

Admiral, Vice Admiral, Rear Admiral

Admiral (or other rank) Evelyn S. Dwain, USN
United States Naval Academy

Dear Admiral Dwain:

Commodore, Captain, Commander, Lieutenant Commander
Commodore (or other rank) Justine A. West, USCG

Dear Commodore (or other rank) West:

Junior Officers: Lieutenant, Lieutenant Junior Grade, Ensign
Ensign (or other rank) Winona B. Tucker, USN
USS Yorktown

Dear Ms. Tucker:

Chief Warrant Officer, Warrant Officer
Warrant Officer (or Chief Warrant Officer) Kevin C. Costello, USCG
USS Saratoga

Dear Mr. Costello:

Chaplain
Chaplain Norman I. O'Keane
Department of the Navy

Dear Chaplain O'Keane:

UNITED NATIONS OFFICIALS

The United Nations is composed of six branches: the General Assembly, the Security Council, the Economic and Social Council, the Trusteeship Council, the International Court of Justice, and the Secretariat.

Secretary General, Under Secretary

His Excellency, Ashok Nalamwar
Secretary General of the United Nations
The Secretariat
United Nations

Formal	*Informal*
Excellency:	Dear Mr. Secretary General:

The Honorable Jean-Paul DuMare
Under Secretary of the United Nations
The Secretariat
United Nations

Formal	*Informal*
Sir:	Dear Mr. DuMare: *OR*
	Dear Under Secretary
	DuMare:

Foreign Representative—Ambassador Rank

His Excellency Eduardo Costa-Graves
Representative of Uruguay to the United Nations

Formal	*Informal*
Excellency:	Dear Mr. Ambassador:

U.S. Representative—Ambassador Rank

U.S. citizens, regardless of rank in the United Nations, are never addressed as *Excellency*.

The Honorable Cecilia N. McIntee
United States Representative to the United Nations

Formal	*Informal*
Madam:	Dear Madam Ambassador:

PART

Two

MODEL LETTERS

CHAPTER
≡FIVE

SOCIAL LETTERS

Social correspondence means letters, invitations, and announcements written to family and friends. These messages help you keep in touch with those who mean the most to you. They are your half of a written conversation. As such, they should convey news about what is happening in your life, what is important to you, and what aspects of your personal growth and activities might interest your friends and family.

In turn, social letters and notes offer an opportunity to respond to messages you have received, to affirm ties of affection and respect, and to find out what is happening in the lives of those you love. The following guidelines offer tips on how to make your social correspondence a true reflection of your personality.

ANNOUNCEMENTS

Announcements may be formal, as in an engraved engagement announcement, or informal, as in a letter. Follow the inverted pyramid structure, in which you state the important news first and mention details second. Double-check your facts before sending out the message. If you are announcing the start of a new business, for example, make sure the address and telephone number are correct. Attention to details makes all the difference in this type of message.

Engagement (See also Weddings)

Engagements may be announced informally through letters to family and friends or through a formal announcement in the newspaper and through the mail to family and friends.

Informal:

May 12, 19--

Dear Lorraine,

I wanted you to be the first in the family to know—since you were the one to introduce me to Cecilia. I asked her to marry me last night and she said yes! I can't believe, after working up my nerve for two days, that she accepted. It looks like a December wedding, when she gets back from New York.

I know you'll want to be in on the wedding plans. Cecilia already has a list of things for her friends to do. Thanks for introducing me to the person I fell in love with.

Love,

Bruce

Bruce

Dear Mom and Dad,

Remember after you met Bruce you told me, "You're a fool if you let this one get away"? Well, I didn't! Last night he asked me to marry him and I said yes! I don't think my feet have hit the ground yet. He bought me a gorgeous solitaire diamond—the kind I have wanted since I was a girl.

I'm so happy, Mom and Dad, especially since I know you like Bruce as well. We are planning on a December wedding when I get back from New York. Bruce starts with his new company in the spring, so we'll be staying in the area for at least another four years. I'll call you as soon as I get home—we have a million things to do!

Love,

Cecilia

Cecilia

It is customary for the parents of the bride to make the formal announcement, either to the newspaper or on engraved stationery by mail. The correct form and wording for a formal engagement announcement is as follows:

Formal:

Mr. Eugene Dickerson and Ms. Anabelle Lark-Dickerson
have the honor to announce
the engagement of their daughter
Cecilia Anne
to
Mr. Bruce C. Westlake

If for any reason the engagement is broken, the change should be announced to all those who received the original notice. The announcement would read:

Mr. Eugene Dickerson and Ms. Annabelle Lark-Dickerson
wish to announce
that the engagement of their daughter
Cecilia Anne
and
Mr. Bruce C. Westlake
has been broken by mutual consent

Even if the consent was not mutual, stating so saves everyone's face.

New Baby

Birth announcements are sent to family and friends after the event and as soon as everyone is sure both mother and child (or children) are doing fine. Stationery stores have several styles of birth announcement cards. You may prefer to design your own or simply write a letter announcing the news.

March 13, 19--

Dear Sam and Pauline,

On March 12, at 6:32 am, you became aunt and uncle to a beautiful baby girl, 8 pounds, 7 ounces! The delivery was so fast we didn't even have time to get to the delivery room, and I gave birth to her in the elevator! We nicknamed her "Speedy." I thought the doctor was going to faint, he was so flustered.

Her official name is Maxine Sharon, after both our maternal grandmothers. Please come to see her as soon as you can. I want her to meet her Aunt Pauline and Uncle Sam.

Love,

Pam

Pam

A traditional formal birth announcement follows this format:

Mr. and Mrs. Morton A. Bernstein
take pleasure in announcing
the birth of a daughter
Maxine Sharon
on Tuesday, March 12, 19--

Today, baby announcements are not reserved only for births to couples. More single men and women and married couples are adopting children, and single women are having children on their own. You can send an adoption or single-parent birth announcement in place of a regular birth announcement. The top line states the name of the individual or couple involved, while the last two lines give the name and age of the child.

Mr. Fred C. Holling
is happy and proud to announce
the adoption of
Christopher Robert
age, eight months

Divorce

Although divorce is generally a painful process, you need to notify friends and relatives about the event. If you are not up to writing a letter, you can send a printed card with your change of name or address, then add a personal note regarding the divorce. A letter can let people know you still want to keep in touch with them.

Printed Card

Ingrid Quist
(formerly Mrs. Lars Ericsson)
has changed her address to
2434 Archer Drive
Columbus, Ohio 43228

I'll be moving next week —Lars & I have decided this is best,

Ingrid

Letter

Dear Peggy and Bert,

I know you would rather hear it from me than from someone else—Lars and I finally gave up trying to make our marriage work. The divorce was granted July 10. This is a painful time for both of us, but we decided it was best to let each other go.

I just want to say that your friendship means the world to me, and your support throughout our struggle has been deeply appreciated. I'll be moving to the new address (see card enclosed) this week. I hope to have you over as soon as I can. Love you both dearly.

My dear friends,

Ingrid

Ingrid

Death Notice

Newspapers feature an obituary column where notices of deaths are printed. The announcement must be made immediately after the death; if you don't have time to mail the notice, you can hand deliver it or read it over the phone. The format for a death notice follows:

MISZEWSKI—Stanley R. Miszewski, on November 24, 19--. Loving husband of Krystyna Guszak, beloved father of Irene and Chester. Funeral services Thursday, November 26, 3 pm at Schierer Funeral Parlor, 1342 Maple, Traverse City. Flowers welcome or send a contribution to the National Cancer Institute.

A letter announcing the death of a friend or relative is a courtesy to people who knew the deceased. It gives them an opportunity to attend services if they wish or to send their condolences to the family.

November 24, 19--

Dear Mr. Waugh:

It is with great sadness that I must tell you that my father died this morning in Van Buren Memorial Hospital. He was undergoing a fairly complex operation and his heart failed. The medical team was unable to revive him. We are all still dealing with the shock.

My father spoke of you fondly through the years, and I know he treasured the time the two of you spent in law school. We thought you would want to know of his death as soon as possible.

We will be conducting a memorial service for all those people who cannot make it to the funeral. The service will be held at First Baptist Church in Bellingham, on Thursday, November 29, 19-- at 10:30 am. We hope you can come and share your memories of our father.

With fond regards,

Art Takehara

Art Takehara

New Business Venture

Launching a new business is an exciting event. You want the world to know about it—or at the very least your family, friends, and neighbors, who may be potential customers. New business announcements may take a variety of forms—brochures, printed cards, newsletters, letters, or flyers. This type of announcement lends itself to the question-and-answer format. You need to ask yourself what the recipient should know about your business or service.

A sample of a letter announcement is given below:

MSC TUTORING SERVICES

Stuart A. Streiber, MS, PhD

1543 Crain Ave.

Everett, Louisiana 70639

(412) 556-3211

Dear Friends:

I am pleased to announce that beginning August 1, I am offering elementary, high school, and college level tutoring in math, sciences, and computers (MSC). As a former math teacher, I have over 12 years experience teaching students at all levels of ability.

I offer the following services to students:
— Basic math and science principles
— Good study habits
— How to identify strengths and weaknesses
— How to take standardized tests.

I believe in teaching the whole person, not just academic subjects. Students have the intelligence to learn—they often need someone who believes in their ability.

If your son or daughter needs extra help before or during the school year, call now. Tutoring times and fees are arranged on an individual basis.

Sincerely,

Stuart A. Streiber

Stuart A. Streiber

Graduation

Graduation from high school or college marks a milestone in any young person's life. He or she is making the transition from childhood to adulthood, and the occasion deserves to be celebrated. Graduation announcements can be informal or printed on engraved stationery. Often, formal announcements include an invitation to a reception or party after the graduation ceremony.

Informal Letter

Dear Aunt Thelma and Uncle Bill,

It is with great pride and relief that we announce our son Rudy's upcoming high school graduation. We thought for awhile he would not pass math, but we found a super tutor, Stuart Streiber, who turned Rudy around.

We are so proud of Rudy for his hard work. He has matured so much in his senior year that he is truly a young man now, no longer a child.

Graduation ceremonies will take place on June 12, 19--, in the gymnasium of East Trenton High School, at 2:00 pm. We are planning a family dinner afterwards and would love to have you come. I know Rudy would like to see you there to help him celebrate his achievement.

Best wishes,

Lorna Hamil

Lorna Hamil

A formal graduation announcement is sent to family, friends, business associates, and others who may know your offspring and wish to be included in the occasion.

Mr. and Mrs. Leonard S. Walker
are proud to announce
the graduation of their daughter
Gail Irene
from the University of Illinois
on
Tuesday, 3:00 PM, June 2, 19--
Ceremony to take place at Fisk Hall,
2453 Sheridan Road, Champaign-Urbana

A card inviting people to a reception or party afterward may have the following format:

You are invited to a reception
following the graduation ceremony
to be held at 243 Ashley Drive, Urbana
from 5:00 pm to 8:00 pm
RSVP

APOLOGIES

Even the best of us make mistakes, fail to keep our promises, or allow situations to get out of hand. When these things happen, an apology is in order. But you want to write an apology that avoids aggravating the situation. Follow these guidelines for sending an effective apology.

▶ Explain briefly how the mistake happened and apologize sincerely. Lengthy explanations sound like elaborate excuses and are not needed. Similarly, exaggerated apologies sound insincere and can add fuel to a smoldering fire.

▶ Assure the recipient that you value his or her goodwill.

▶ If appropriate, tell the recipient how you will guard against future mistakes.

Forgotten Events

Nearly everyone likes to be remembered on a birthday, anniversary, or other important date. But at times, these dates may slip your mind, and you must send belated greetings. If your message is a gift, include an apology note as a courtesy to the recipient.

October 24, 19--

Dear Bill,

In all the rush to meet my deadlines, I inadvertently let one of the most important dates — your birthday — slip past me. Please forgive my belated gift. It carries no less good wishes for being late.

I hope you had a wonderful birthday. Your friendship means so much to everyone who knows you. Please accept my apologies again for the lateness of my birthday greetings. I've programmed all special dates into my computer calendar — so no chance your birthday will slip by again!

Warmest regards,
Aisha

Canceled Plans

At one time or another, you will have to cancel plans made with other people. If you must cancel at the last minute, follow up with an apology. A short note can do much to restore good feeling between you and the ones you must disappoint or inconvenience.

February 16, 19--

Dear Francine,

I apologize again for the last-minute cancellation of our Valentine's Day plans. You had put so much work into arranging the party — I felt very bad about having to fly to New York on company business at the last minute.

I hope these flowers can do a little to make up for the disappointment. Let's plan to take that trip we've been talking about — just the two of us.

All my love,
Marty

Misunderstanding

Misunderstandings can lead to a serious rupture in relationships if they are not cleared up quickly. In the apology, take responsibility for your part of the misunderstanding without judging or blaming the other person. The only behavior you can change or control is your own. Suggest a way that future misunderstandings can be avoided.

May 23, 19--

Dear Angie,

I feel terrible. I could have sworn you said you'd pick up the kids after the school basketball game—I guess I was wrong and I apologize. It's a good thing you had the foresight to make sure that your son Robby always has enough money for a phone call. Thanks for dropping everything at the last minute and driving over to the school to pick up Robby and my boys.

What do you think about the idea of making up a car pool schedule for the rest of the games? That way we'll always know whose turn it is to pick up the boys. Let's talk about it, okay? Once again, thanks for filling in for me.

Your friend,

Robyn

Robyn

CONGRATULATIONS

People appreciate recognition for their achievements. When something special occurs in the life of someone you know, send a congratulatory message as soon as possible. Focus on the special event without bringing in other news. The message can be brief and sincere. Depending on the situation, handwrite or type the letter on personalized or business stationery.

Engagement and Marriage

Express your best wishes to the couple even if you aren't particularly pleased about the partner the man or woman has chosen. You could be wrong, and by holding your peace, you give yourself a chance to reverse your opinion gracefully. If you send best wishes to one of an engaged couple, ask him or her to pass along your congratulations to the other person. Traditionally, you congratulate the man and extend best wishes to the woman on the occasion of an engagement or marriage.

Engagement

June 14, 19--

Dear Cecilia,

What great news about your engagement! Now I can tell you that Aunt Ethel and I have been secretly hoping for some time that you and Bruce would take the step. You seemed to be so well suited to each other.

Bruce is a fine young man, Cecilia, and he's lucky to be marrying such a bright, talented young woman as you. Best wishes to you both from a doting aunt and uncle. May you enjoy every happiness and success in your life together.

Affectionately,

Uncle Bert and Aunt Ethel

Wedding

January 15, 19--

Dear Cecilia and Bruce,

Congratulations and best wishes to you both on your wedding! I understand you had a beautiful December ceremony at St. Bartholomew's. Please accept my best wishes for every happiness. I'm only sorry we couldn't make it to the wedding.

When you get to New York next fall, please look us up. We'll celebrate in style.

With warmest regards,

Carl and Alicia Hansen

Wedding Anniversary

Either a handwritten note or a printed card with an additional note is appropriate for wedding anniversaries. If the year is a special one (ten, fifteen, twenty-five, fifty), mention it in the message. If you know one of the partners better than the other, you may write to him or her, extending best wishes to both partners in your letter.

June 18, 19--

Dear Ralph and Orleen,

Congratulations on your twenty-fifth wedding anniversary! I remember so well the university chapel where you were married, and it doesn't seem that long ago.

You have had so many wonderful years together—I can only wish you more of the same ahead. Happy anniversary.

Love,

Rose and Karl

Rose and Karl

Birth of a Child

Usually, you will write this message in response to a birth announcement. Reply immediately either with a handwritten message or a note written in a printed card.

May 27, 19--

Dear Juana,

How happy and proud you must be to have such a beautiful baby girl. Congratulations! From the photo you sent, I can see she has your blue eyes and Tony's dark hair. She's perfectly lovely, Juana.

Let me know when you decide on a name. And call when you feel up to having visitors — I'd love to see her for myself! All my best to you and Tony.

Love,

Aunt Maria

Graduation

Graduation is a special highwater mark in a young person's life. In your message, comment on any special effort or achievements the graduate made during his or her high school or college career.

June 14, 19--

Dear Sandra,

Congratulations on receiving your law degree. You've worked hard for this moment, and you must be very proud. Marvin and I have watched you grow from a tomboyish little girl next door into a poised, confident young woman. We feel an almost parental pride on your graduation day.

Congratulations again on your remarkable achievement. We know that your career will benefit from the same commitment and effort that you devoted to your academic work. We wish you the best!

Warmest regards,

Marvin & Shana Levy

Award or Honor

When someone wins an award or honor, your letter of congratulation should state the award received and mention the qualities of the person you feel helped earn the honor.

May 24, 19--

Dear Ms. Paolucci,

Many congratulations on being named Teacher of the Year. You were certainly my first choice. The extra attention you've given our daughter Julie in her math lessons really helped her. In one year she went from a D to a B +, and the difference in her self-confidence is amazing. She actually thinks math can be fun!

We owe it all to your kindness and skill. I've heard other parents sing your praises as well. The children are fortunate to have a teacher of your patience and experience in the classroom. To my husband and me, you will always be Teacher of the Year.

Warmest regards,

Mrs. Claire Begosion

Mrs. Claire Begosian

Promotion/Career Achievement

Career advancements mean a lot to the person receiving them, and they mean even more when they are recognized by family and friends. Send the person a brief, sincere note of congratulation for the accomplishment.

March 22, 19--

Dear Karen,

I just learned from your mother about your promotion to general manager at Reital Corporation. My heartfelt congratulations on your achievement. I always knew you had the intelligence and drive to go far, and you keep proving me right time and again.

You have excellent managerial qualities—I still remember all those cookie sales you organized when you were only 10 or 11 years old. I'm glad the management at Reital recognizes your abilities. Best wishes for your continued success.

Sincerely,

Pierre Simone

Pierre Simone

FAMILY

Correspondence between family members is generally informal and concerned primarily with personal affairs—sharing news, expressing feelings, talking about children, and other mutual concerns. Be sure that you extend to your family the same courtesies you give your friends. Try to answer letters promptly when someone expresses a concern or asks questions.

A good rule of thumb is to keep your correspondence sincere, saying only what genuinely expresses your feelings. If you find it difficult to write to some family members, keep your letters brief and neutral. Save your more intimate details for family members with whom you have a stronger relationship.

Adult Child Away from Home

Whether the adult child is away on a trip or has moved to another city, a letter from home can be a welcome sight in the mailbox. The one receiving the letter will want to know all the news, what's happening at home to friends, to other family members. Even adult children want to know they are missed, so be liberal in sharing your affection.

Above all, avoid offering unsolicited advice, complaining, nagging, scolding, or otherwise bringing the tone and content of the letter down to a depressing level. Instead, show interest in what interests them—surroundings, work, outside activities, friends, and other highlights.

May 22, 19--

Dearest Rosa,

I hope you are settled into your new home by now. We miss you very much. It seems strange not to hear you rustling about the house—and to have a nearly silent phone. You make the place so lively when you're here!

Thanks so much for the pictures of your house. I love the screened-in porch on the front and the small garden to the side.

Could you use those white wicker chairs that Dad wanted to get rid of? We could send them with Luis the next time he drives out your way—he has a new truck that he loves to show off. He's never volunteered to do so many driving and hauling chores in his life!

How has the job turned out? I know you were so excited about starting in advertising as a copywriter. I hope you find new friends at the agency quickly—although I shouldn't worry. You've been able to make good friends wherever you went.

One sober note—Dad is going in for a biopsy of his left lung—the doctor found a mass when they took an X ray last Tuesday. The surgeon doing the procedure is one of the best in the country, so we're thankful for that. Your father has everyone puzzled—he's never smoked and never worked around asbestos, so no one can figure out where this mass came from.

Yolanda and Linda send their love; they miss you, too. They said the lunch counter at Alfredo's isn't the same since you aren't there to stop by every day.

In case I haven't said it before—you are a real source of pride and joy for all of us. Even though I miss you, it's so good to see you launch into a more adult world for yourself. I know you'll use your good sense when it comes to relationships—we've had enough talks about the risks and rewards of being single that I think you could counsel people twice your age.

Everyone sends their love. Write when you get the chance or give us a call. Go after whatever life has to offer you—make the most of it!

Love,

Mama

Mama

Parents from Adult Child

The same general rules hold for adult children writing to their parents. Parents like to hear some details about their children's lives without necessarily having to know everything. Share what you feel is appropriate, given your situation, and let them know every now and then what you appreciate or miss about them.

August 27, 19--

Dear Dad,

You must be really happy now that the golf course down the road is finished. The guys at work can't believe you have a course within walking distance. They want to know how they can get into Mueller Retirement Community early.

I know you had some real misgivings about giving up the house after Mom died and moving into the Community. It was one of the hardest decisions I've ever seen you make, and I hope, when my time comes to do it, I'll be able to manage as well. One of the things I've always admired about you is your ability to adjust to changes.

In some ways, I wish I could take an early retirement and join you on the golf course. But until the last of the kids is through college, we can't even begin to think of it.

Speaking of the kids, all three are planning to invade the Community at spring break to see you. You might warn the neighbors about it and find out if the local grocery store delivers. They're at the age when they eat anything that stands still. You won't believe how Kirsten has grown. She's nearly six feet now and loves playing on the basketball team at U of C. She's a real jock. Leo is more interested in filming events—his dream is to be a television biggie, as he says. And as for Peggy, she just wants to raise quarterhorses some day.

Trish and I are fine—getting a little slower and a little more forgetful. The kids have a great time teasing us about it. One thing I better mention before I forget. Bob Rostov, the lawyer, wants you to stop by the next time you visit us and check over the estate papers. He said he had a few things to talk to you about—nothing urgent, but he wanted to talk in person to clear up some loose ends from Mom's estate.

By the way, why not try to make it here the week of July 22–28? The kids will be in Ann Arbor then, and we could have a chance to catch up. What do you say?

Take care of yourself. Don't get that handicap too high—I don't have as much chance to practice.

Your son,

Ken

Ken

Hurt Feelings Between Relatives

Family relationships are highly vulnerable to misunderstandings, jealousies, competition, and the like. Unless such situations are dealt with in a timely manner, they can become deep, lasting divisions that split families and create permanent hard feelings.

You may have occasion to write to someone who has hurt you or write to someone who has been hurt by you. These letters are tricky to compose. Follow these general guidelines.

1. State clearly what the situation was that provoked your feelings.

2. State how you felt—avoid "you" statements and concentrate on "I" statements ("When we fought, I felt *I* had not been heard," *not* "When we fought, I felt *you* didn't listen to me").

3. State, if possible, what you would like to do differently, or what you would like the other person to do differently. Be specific and give them *doable* tasks. Not "I want our relationship to be better," which is much too vague, but "I would like you to really listen to me when I'm giving my side of the story."

4. Keep the letter brief and to the point. Avoid going into exhaustive detail or berating the recipient with a list of past offenses.

5. Realize that you cannot control how people will react to your letter. You can only state your feelings and what you would like. If it is not possible to get what you want, then you have the choice of reducing the amount of time you spend with the person or communicating in another way—by letter or telephone conversation, for example.

February 3, 19--

Dear Andy,

This is a tough letter to write, because usually we get along so well. But at Fran's birthday party, I have to admit that I got really upset when you put my gift behind the door and forgot about it until the last minute. I felt left out of the celebration and that hurt a lot.

I know you've been going through a lot lately, and I hope we can talk about this. I'd like to straighten things out, so we don't have this kind of thing happening again. I'll give you a call this week — you're my only brother and I don't want a wall between us like Dad and his sister have.

Love,
Jillian

When writing to relatives who have been hurt by others, state briefly how you feel about what happened and sympathize with their situation. Avoid castigating the offending party—often it merely pours oil on the fire. If appropriate, offer to talk over the situation or volunteer a sympathetic shoulder.

April 27, 19--

Dear Bridie,

I realize you were deeply hurt by the terms of your father's will. I truly wish there was some way they could be changed.

I'm quite sure he intended no slight; he's simply from a generation that doesn't think about women as breadwinners or heads of households. In his view, daughters have someone to look after them, while sons need all the money to raise their families. He was wrong about that, and if he had had our experiences, he would have had a different outlook.

I hope this won't drive a wedge between you and your brother's family. Money so often divides families. Whenever you're feeling really steamed about all this, why not call me, and we can talk about it.

Your cousin,

Sean

FRIENDS

Letters to and from friends are a running dialogue that keeps you both abreast of what is happening in your lives, how you feel, what changes occur. Friends want to know not only *what is happening* but *what you are feeling*. In your description of a camping trip, for example, include your reactions to what you did and saw, as well as a newsy report on where you went and what activities you experienced.

Friends Back Home

When you have moved or are taking a trip, use your letters to give friends a vivid sense of your new place. Try to make them see, smell, taste, and feel your surroundings. Don't fill your letter with questions about what is happening back home. Instead, let them share in your experience.

February 24, 19--

Dear Bess,

This is our fourth day in Anguilla, and I finally have a chance to write you. I love the Caribbean climate, even if it is a bit humid. The sun soaks right into your bones without burning. I can feel the chill of our Midwestern winters slowly thawing out of my blood.

The guide we've hired to take us around the island in his taxi tells us that the sun's kinder now during the rainy season. (The rain here is wonderful, too, by the way. The sun hides behind a few clouds and then a misty rain starts to fall. Suddenly the sun bursts out, flooding the land with a kind of silvery light. The misty air glitters with rainbows. Then the clouds race off, and we see a clear, golden tropical sunset each night.)

Speaking of water, we went snorkeling our second day. Salim's an old hand at it, but this was only my second time. The first time was in Hawaii, where the sea bottom is clean, white sand with immaculate spots of fine coral and brilliantly colored fish — they swim right up to you! But in Anguilla, snorkeling is a bit spooky. Strange growths of wrinkled, withered-looking coral three to four feet across cover the sea floor. They look like brains —they're even called "brain coral."

Well, maybe I should just stay on the beach from now on! I have to sign off now. Salim and I are going to visit some of the local markets — I'll see if I can find that hat you wanted. Say "hi" to everyone there. We've taken a lot of pictures, so we can give you a guided tour when we get back. See you soon.

Love,
Leann and Salim

Friends Far Away

When friends move away or travel far from home, they want to hear all the news that has happened in their absence. Make sure you give enough detail to satisfy their curiosity and their need to maintain ties to home.

August 13, 19--

Dear Ozzie,

Things have been plenty busy in Muskogee since you left. The biggest news is the drought—we've had no rain since June and everything is withering in the field. Stu Blandick says that unless next year is better, he's going to have to sell his farm. There's even talk of hiring a Navajo rainmaker—I wouldn't be surprised if the town council did.

Trisha and Jodie got married last week—you were right about Jodie getting what he wanted. He worked on Trisha's father until the old man had to say yes just to get him off the place. The wedding was held at night because the days are too hot—we hit 110° the day they got married.

Oh, some couple from Boynton bought your uncle's place. They're newlyweds, Uncle Cruse said. They plan on fixing it up and starting an antique and pottery store for the tourist trade in the fall. I guess the wife makes pots and dishes out of clay—who knows, they might make it.

One good thing about the drought—I haven't had to get the roof fixed! We're going to wait until September when the government money comes. Then I can get the kind of tar paper you recommended. Your nephew Shane is going to help me—that boy has got a natural touch for carpentry work.

Well, give my regards to Ella and your daughters. We sure miss you. Write if you get a chance. If you want to get away from the city for awhile, you know you've got a place to stay here.

Your friend,

Chuck
Chuck

Explaining Why You Haven't Written

You suddenly realize it's been three months since you received a friend's letter, and you still haven't written back. If you don't have time to write at length, at least get a short note off to let him or her know you haven't forgotten. Explain briefly why you haven't written, include a few lines about your life, and end with an intention to write more or some other indication that you value the friendship.

October 22, 19--

Dear Katie,

After all this time since your last letter, you must think I've dropped off the end of the world. It's just that things have been so hectic since September, getting four kids settled in school and then Patrick's accident two weeks ago. I haven't had time to do much beyond make it from one day to the next.

Patrick wasn't hurt, thank God, but our car was completely totaled—which has been a real hardship for me and the kids. Some poor kid who just got his license ran a stop light and broad-sided Patrick at thirty miles an hour. That husband of mine has some kind of protective charm; he walked away without a scratch.

Anyway, I loved getting your letter—it means so much to me that we still keep in touch after all these years. When I get another breather I'll write more. I just wanted to get this note off before any more time went by. Hope you and the kids are well—give Greg a hug for me.

Love,

Lucille

Lucille

Asking Why Someone Hasn't Written

You may find yourself on the other end of the stick—waiting to get a letter in response to one you have written to a friend. You can opt for a serious inquiry or take a humorous tack. Either way, assume that the friend's intentions are good or that something may be preventing him or her from writing.

March 4, 19--

Dear Rick,

If you don't write soon, I'm going to need a new mailbox. Mine is getting worn out from all the times I check it for a letter from you.

Seriously, I hope things are all right there in Chicago. I always look forward to your letters — it's almost like being there with you.

How about dropping a line — save an innocent mailbox!

Sincerely,
Cal

Visits with Friends

One of the pleasures of life is visiting with friends, especially those you haven't seen in some time. The most common letters are invitations for friends to visit you or requests by you to visit them. Offer specific dates and times for visits so your friends will know how to arrange their schedule around your visit or arrange their plans to visit you. Also, make sure you give people ample time to adjust their plans.

Planning to Come

June 23, 19--

Dear Jim,

I'm taking a vacation August 17–31, and I plan to spend it driving along the East Coast seeing the sights. I'll be in Maine August 23–25, and would like to stop by and see you if you're going to be around those days.

We could try out that new boat you got last year. Let me know if August 23–25 is good for you.

Sincerely,

Sol

Sol

Invitation to Visit

November 23, 19--

Dear Ramon and Luz,

Since you're going to be laid over in Dallas on December 15, why not stay in town another day or two and catch a flight out on Wednesday, instead of Monday? We haven't seen each other in four years—and there's a lot of catching up to do!

We can show you around our city—they have some of the best Tex-Mex restaurants here. I know how Ramon likes his hot sauces. What do you say? Get in on Monday morning, stay over two days, and fly out Wednesday. Think it over. We'd love to have you as our guests. We've got plenty of room.

Love,

Sid + Bonita

Sid and Bonita

HOLIDAYS

Holidays provide an opportunity to keep in touch with others, either through newsy letters or brief notes written on commercial cards. Today, commercial cards cover nearly every occasion from Christmas and Hanukkah to Mother's Day, Father's Day, Halloween, and Thanksgiving.

Through the years, greeting card companies have expanded their holiday lines to give people a wide range of choices from the highly religious to the highly secular. You should be able to find the card that best expresses your sentiments, adding a few brief words of your own.

If, as happens in many families, your family relations are strained or distant, keep your greetings brief but sincere. Neutral expressions such as "Holiday greetings to everyone there," or "I wish you a happy holiday" adequately cover the occasion.

Christmas/Hanukkah

Christmas and Hanukkah are widely celebrated by both religious and nonreligious communities. Your greetings can be tailored to the personal beliefs of your recipients. For some people, a religious card is appropriate. For others, the message "Seasons Greetings" or "Holiday Wishes" is more suitable. Be sensitive to your recipients' wishes.

For many people, these holidays are a good chance to tell others about family or personal activities. A printed or mimeographed "Christmas letter" often accompanies the traditional Christmas card to family and friends.

The examples below are appropriate either as separate notes by themselves or as handwritten additions to a commercial card.

Religious

Dear Barbara, Stuart, and family,

May this time of our Savior's birth bring you joy and good health throughout the coming year. We wish we could be with you to celebrate this holiday time. Maybe next year we can all gather here.

Love to you all,
Wilma and Dan

Nonreligious

Dear Gerda and Richard,

Just a note to say I wish you both a very Happy Hanukkah and a happy, healthy, prosperous New Year. We are looking forward to better times—may this coming year be the best one ever.

Love,

Elke

Elke

New Year

No matter which New Year you celebrate—Western calendar, traditional Asian calendar, Rosh Hashanah—the traditional wish for New Year's Day is for health, prosperity, and general good fortune. Most people regard this day as a ''fresh start'' for the upcoming year.

Dear Cindy and Everett,

With 19–– fast approaching, we wish you both all the best and a very Happy New Year. May this year bring health, prosperity, and peace to us all.

Warm regards,

Flora & Seymour

Flora and Seymour

Easter/Passover

Like Christmas, Easter is widely celebrated as a secular as well as religious holiday. Easter greetings in commercial cards range from devotional to strictly secular. Let the individual needs of the recipients dictate which type of message you send.

The Feast of Passover (Pesach) commemorates the Jewish people's flight from Egypt. Although many people send messages only at Hanukkah, Passover is also a time for sending greetings.

Easter

Dear Wayne and family,

Good wishes for a happy Easter — may you enjoy this day and have fun hunting all those eggs we dyed this week! See you soon.

Love,
Aunt May and Uncle Norman

Passover

Dear Leonard and Sheila,

From all of us here in Miami, we wish you and the family a joyous Pesach celebration. May God's love bless you, dear ones, and make your lives long and happy.

Love,
Harriet and Aaron, David, Ariel, and Troy

Thanksgiving

The traditional message at this time of year reaffirms family ties or expresses regret at not being able to gather with friends and family. Commercial cards for this holiday run the gamut from humorous to devotional.

Dear Grandma and Grandpa,

Have a great Thanksgiving. I wish I could be there with you. I remember so many good times at your house on Thanksgiving Day. Remember the time Chris and I ate a whole pumpkin pie before dinner? Say hello to all the cousins, and give my newest niece a hug for me. Hope you all have a wonderful day.

Love,
Yoshi

INVITATIONS

Invitations can be formal or informal. Formal invitations are written in the third person ("Mr. and Mrs. Levitt request the pleasure of your company . . ."). They may be handwritten on fine stationery or engraved or printed. Formal dress for the event is indicated in the lower right-hand corner. If a reply is required, the abbreviation R.S.V.P. is written in the lower left-hand corner. For faster response, you may want to include a reply card with your invitations.

Informal invitations are written in the first person ("We would like to invite you . . .," "John and I are having a dinner party . . ."). These invitations are usually handwritten on personal stationery. They can be conservative or creative, using unusual shapes, concepts, or decorations. Fill-in cards for parties can be purchased from the local stationery or office supply store.

Dinner—Formal

Formal dinner invitations for an occasion that includes out-of-town guests should be sent two to three months in advance. This gives people time to make travel arrangements. When the dinner is for local guests only, invitations can be sent out three to five weeks before the event. Formal dinners are common in the business world and in political or official government circles.

Some invitations are printed with the recipient's name, but most simply use "you" or "your" in place of a name. The correct phrasing for a formal invitation is " . . . request the pleasure of your company."

Always spell out the time and all names and dates on formal invitations.

Mr. and Mrs. George Giannopoulos
request the pleasure of your company
at dinner
on Thursday, the Fourteenth of April
at half past eight o'clock
1200 South Whitehall Drive
Salem

R.S.V.P.   Black tie

Party Invitations

Birthdays, anniversaries, holidays, and other special events are all occasions for a party. You can exercise your imagination in sending out invitations for parties. One couple wrote their invitations for a Halloween party on the reverse side of candy wrappers. Make sure that in your creative bursts, you don't forget essential information—where, what time, what day, what to bring (if anything), and whether a reply is needed.

Birthday.   Birthday parties are among the most common and most popular of all festive occasions. They serve as a way to introduce young children to the social customs and traditions of your family and the culture. For older children and adults, they mark significant moments when family and friends gather to celebrate another year of life for someone they care about.

On your birthday invitations, be sure to mark clearly any special instructions to your guests—"no gifts please," "donations to _____ charity in lieu of gifts," "bring your favorite toy," "wear casual clothes."

You are invited to a birthday party!

For: *Andy Rubinstein*

Date: *Sunday, May 27*

Time: *8:00 p.m. – ???*

Place: *2214 Maple Avenue, apt 23*

No gifts, please! Bring your favorite sixties records, cassettes, or CDs and be ready to twist the night away!

Wedding Anniversary. Anniversary parties marking special years—tenth, twenty-fifth, fiftieth—generally call for special celebrations. They are a time when the family gathers to honor the achievement of two people living together for so many years. Whether the couple gets along or not, these landmark anniversaries are still an achievement. Invitations for anniversary parties can be formal, on engraved stationery, or informal, a brief letter to friends and family.

As in the birthday invitations, be sure to clearly state any special instructions to your guests on the invitation itself.

> Mark, Sandy, and Gordon Quinn,
> children of Mr. and Mrs. Ira Quinn
> request the pleasure of your company
> at a party celebrating
> their parents' fiftieth wedding anniversary
> on Wednesday, the nineteenth of October
> at seven o'clock
> the Hyatt Regency Hotel
> 2235 West Carlton Avenue
> Dallas

R.S.V.P.   White tie
345-5671

September 15, 19--

Dear Uncle Avery and Aunt Wanda,

Mark, Sandy, and I are planning a real bash for our folks' fiftieth wedding anniversary this October. It's going to be on the 19th at the Hyatt Regency Hotel, 7:00 pm, and we really want you to be there. I hope you can make it.

I know how many stories you've always told us about when Mom and Dad were first married and how much trouble they had rehabbing their first house. Could you write up some of the best stories by the end of this month and send them to me? We want to print them up in a booklet and give them to Mom and Dad.

The three of us are going to do the same—the highlights of our life with them over the past fifty years!

Let me know if you can come to the party and if you can write up the stories.

Affectionately,

Gordon

Gordon

Special Occasions. Graduations, confirmations, bar/bas mitzvahs, end of the school year, finishing a PhD, welcome home—almost any special occasion can serve as the impetus for a party. No matter how creative your invitations, remember to print all essential information clearly.

You're invited to a

Bon Voyage Party for the Myers!

S.S. HONOLULU

Tuesday, February 4

at 8:30pm

at the Brandeaus

415 Golf Road

ALOHA!

Informal invitations can be a brief letter or a fill-in card to your intended guests. Informal invitations are generally written in two paragraphs, the first giving the details of the dinner and the second a personal message to the recipient.

Dear Nancy and Bo,

Stan and I are giving a dinner party next Friday, the 12th of May, at eight o'clock. We would love to have the two of you with us.

We have a lot to talk about since you got back from Washington, D.C. We do hope you can come.

Sincerely,

Amy O'Brien

Amy O'Brien

Recalling an Invitation. Unexpected news can cause the best-laid plans to be cancelled. If you have time to send a printed cancellation, use either the word *recall* or *cancel* in your message. If possible, mention that you will set another date for the dinner. The recall message should follow the format of the original invitation.

In most cases, if you have to cancel an informal dinner, you simply telephone your guests and tell them in person. If for some reason you can't call, then write a brief message indicating the reason for the cancellation and whether the dinner will be rescheduled.

Dear Nancy and Bo,

Because of an unexpected illness in the family, Stan and I will have to cancel our dinner party on the 12th of May. We are very sorry to have to disappoint everyone.

We will try to reschedule our dinner when we return. I hope we can arrange a convenient date for everyone!

Regretfully,

Amy O'Brien

Amy O'Brien

Cancelling a Party.   Party invitations can be cancelled by telephone or a written note. If you can reschedule or move the party to another location, indicate this in the message.

February 12, 19--

Dear Friends,

A burst water main on our street flooded our basement and has forced us to cancel our party for the 14th.

However, the Holloways have graciously offered their home as an alternative site. So our party will move to the Holloways, 22435 South Terrace Dr., on the 15th, at 7:30 pm. I don't know about you, but we can sure use a good party! Hope to see you all there.

Sincerely,

Frieda Schmidt

Frieda Schmidt

Showers

Showers can run the gamut from formal sit-down dinners to informal gatherings at the office. The nature of the gathering will determine the type of invitation you send. Showers are generally built around a theme—baby showers, china showers, wedding showers—and should be specified in the invitation. If you want the shower to be a surprise, mention this in your message to ensure secrecy.

May 15, 19--

Dear Ms. Carrell,

My sister and I are giving a kitchen shower for Teresa on Sunday, June 12, at 12:00 pm. I hope you will be able to attend and stay for a buffet luncheon afterward.

Please bring any items that you feel would grace a newly-wed's kitchen. Teresa mentioned that she doesn't have any good cooking ware or everyday dishes.

The shower is a surprise, so if you see Teresa before Sunday, please don't say anything to her. We are looking forward to meeting you—Teresa has mentioned often how kind you have been to her.

Sincerely yours,

Jewel and Lilly Mae Brewer

Jewel and Lilly Mae Brewer

Replying to Invitations

The first cardinal rule in responding to invitations is to reply promptly! This not only ensures that your host or hostess knows whether you are coming but also helps guarantee that you will put the event on your calendar right away.

The second cardinal rule is to respond with a definite yes or no. Don't give your host or hostess a vague "we-might-or-might-not-be-coming" answer. State clearly whether you will be able to come to the dinner, party, christening, or other occasion.

If the R.S.V.P. lists a telephone number, call in your acceptance or regrets; do not send a written note. If there is no indication that the host or hostess needs a written or personal response, then you are not required to reply. However, if you can't attend, telling the host or hostess is a thoughtful act.

Accepting Invitations.   To accept a formal invitation, imitate the wording in your reply. If the invitation reads, for example, "celebrate our son's graduation," then write "celebrate with you."

We will be delighted
to celebrate with you
on Friday, the thirteenth of June
Amy Price and Ilene Jefferson

For informal invitations, write a brief letter in reply.

July 15, 19--

Dear Frieda and Hans,

We will be happy to come to your party — it sounds like you could use some fun in your life after the water disaster.

We've marked the date on our calendar. Let us know if we can bring anything.

Sincerely,
Lorraine and Hank Ross

Declining Invitations.   When declining formal invitations, use the same format as the acceptance, substituting a "regret" line.

When declining an informal invitation, use the diamond sequence. Mention your pleasure or honor at being invited, your reason for declining, and then your regrets. If appropriate, suggest another time you might get together and mention you would appreciate being kept in mind for future events.

November 2, 19--

Dear Gina,

I was looking forward very much to being with you on the 13th at your dinner party. Unfortunately, I learned today that the company is sending me to Argentina on business that week. So it is with considerable regret that I must decline your invitation.

Thank you for asking me, and I hope you'll give me a chance to say "yes" in the future.

Affectionately,
Robert Houseman

SYMPATHY/CONDOLENCES

When people have sustained a loss or tragedy, whether through death, accident, or illness, the best sympathy or condolence message is brief and sincere. People dealing with grief or shock are often unable to read long letters or to handle an outpouring of "let me tell you about my loss" or "how devastated you must be" from someone else.

Write your sympathy message promptly, as soon as you hear of the event. The wording of your message will depend on how well you know the person you are writing. In general, keep your language simple and clear. State briefly how you feel about the loss, then move on quickly to an expression of sympathy for your reader. If appropriate, end with an offer of help.

Although commercial cards are fine, add a personal note of your own. Often, the recipient may skip the message and read only the name or handwritten note. Personal sympathy cards, even in formal correspondence, should be handwritten. Typewritten or printed sympathy messages are appropriate from a firm or organization.

Deaths

The death of a loved one is the most common occasion eliciting a sympathy message. To avoid unintentionally offending or wounding your reader, follow these simple guidelines.

1. State your shock or sadness at hearing of the death. State briefly what the person meant to you or what you appreciated most or will miss most about the person.

2. Acknowledge the recipient's loss—do not jump immediately to what the person can be thankful for ("He's with God now," "You still have your other children," "She's resting in heaven"). The grieving person is still dealing with the fact their loved one is gone. They may be angry or depressed about the event, and those feelings need to be honored.

3. Avoid saying "Let me know if there's anything I can do." Very often, people in times of grief are unable to reach out or

to state what they need. Take the initiative and offer instead to call later and find out what you can do.

4. Remember that grief is a process, not an event. The grieving person may go through stages of recovery and relapse, particularly around anniversaries of the death date or around the deceased person's birthday, or other important dates. Remember these times with a card or visit. The grieving person may simply need someone to talk with on anniversary or other dates when memories of the deceased are likely to be especially keen.

5. Be supportive, but avoid giving advice, admonitions to "Get on with your life" or "It's time to put this all behind you," or other well-meant but unhelpful actions. Grief—as a process—has its own timetable.

6. Realize that recovery from deep grief, particularly involving the death of a child, can take years. Be sensitive in your subsequent letters or notes to the grieving person by occasionally mentioning that you support their recovery.

Death of a Spouse. The loss of a partner means a sudden and often radical change in the survivor's life. Even if the relationship was not a happy one, the survivor will feel the loss. Recognize this fact in your message by acknowledging the implications of the death for the surviving partner.

May 12, 19--

My dearest Esther,

I was greatly saddened to learn of Benjamin's death. My heart goes out to you at this time. You must miss him very much. In the time of readjustment that lies ahead, please know that you are not alone. I will call you in a few days to see what I can do to help.

Love,
Germaine

Death of a Parent. As the population continues to age and medical care continues to advance, more people will be dealing with a parent's prolonged illness and death. Even after a lengthy illness, however, the finality of death can still come as a shock to the adult children and other relatives.

Be sensitive to this fact when you write your sympathy message. The grieving person may not be feeling relief but a host of other emotions—guilt, fear, denial. Let them know they have your sympathy and support.

January 16, 19--

Dear Tad and Selma,

You have my deepest sympathy for the loss of your father. I understand he had been ill for some time. It must have been difficult for you during these past months.

My thoughts are with you at this time. Your father was one of the kindest men I ever knew. You must miss him very much.

In sympathy,
Fred Huang

Death of a Child. Few events in life are as devastating as the loss of a child. It is not only an individual who has been lost, but a part of a family's future and sense of continuity.

To someone in the midst of grieving for a child who has died, words meant to be comforting—"He (she) is with God now" or "You can always have another child (adopt a child)" or "At least you have the other children"—usually make the situation worse. They do not acknowledge the feelings of the grieving family at the moment. Also, realize that their grief may last for years and may come back with surprising force at various moments—anniversary of the death, the child's birthday, other dates meaningful to the family.

Keep your message brief and sincere. Find out from other family members or friends how you can help.

April 12, 19--

Dear Leah

I still can't believe the news — my heart is filled with sorrow for you and Abe. You are in my prayers these sad days.

My deepest sympathy to everyone in your family. Jay will be greatly missed by all who knew him.

In sympathy,
Eileen

Other Losses

While other losses through accident, illness, natural disasters, and personal disappointments or reverses are not as final as death, they still can hurt. A quick note of condolence or sympathy can help to ease the pain and let people know they are not alone in their troubles.

Accidents.   Injuries are quick to happen, but may be slow to heal. Patients may appreciate sympathy cards during the course of their recovery as well as immediately after the accident occurs.

November 4, 19--

Dear Angie,

Just a quick note to ask how you are doing. Vanessa told me you will be in the hospital for another two weeks. Don't worry about your apartment, we are looking after it—along with Mighty Quinn, who is the smartest dog I've ever met.

Just rest and get better. We miss you at the Center and look forward to having you back. Reba and I will stop by next week to see you.

Warmest regards,

Aretha and Jake
Aretha and Jake

Property Loss. Fire, theft, and natural disasters can wreak havoc with people's property. When someone you know suffers this type of loss, send them a sympathy note to tell them you care.

October 1, 19--

Dear Barry and Sara,

It was really bad luck to have the hurricane hit you so hard. I know how much you love that house. I'm glad the damage wasn't any worse and that neither of you was injured.

I hope that the repairs are going smoothly, and you will soon have your house—and your peace of mind—back in order again. If you need someone to commiserate with you, just call me any-time.

Love,

Annette

Annette

Personal Disappointment or Setback. A kind word in a mo-ment of personal defeat or disappointment is often greatly appreci-ated. In your sympathy message, acknowledge the loss but don't dwell on it or launch into an angry tirade about the unfairness of life. Instead, express confidence in the recipient's abilities and future prospects.

February 9, 19--

Dear Christie,

I'm sorry the job in New York City didn't come through. I know how much you had hoped for it. I'm sure there will be another offer—perhaps even better—in your future. When it happens, let's be sure to celebrate.

Love,

Romana

Romana

Illness. Sympathy cards for this occasion range from the "get-well" variety to condolences for more serious ailments. Make sure you don't assume too much or too little about the nature of the illness. Find out from friends or family members what specific illness the person is suffering and offer your best wishes.

July 17, 19--

Dear Maureen,

I've just learned from Dinah about your diagnosis. It must be hard to adjust to the news right now.

When you are feeling up to it, I'd like to get together with you to see what I can do to help. I don't know very much about multiple sclerosis, but I do know that you are a fighter and have the ability to deal with difficult situations. I'll get in touch with you next week to see how you are doing and when we might get together.

Love,

Tallulah

Tallulah

Divorce. Divorce can be amiable—both parties agree to the breakup—or hotly contested. Regardless, it is a painful time for both parties. Your message to the couple or to either one of the partners will depend on how well you know them. At the very least, an expression of sympathy for the loss of the marriage is appropriate.

March 25, 19--

Dear Morris,

Sorry to learn that you and Golda have divorced. I know you both had hoped your trial separation would help resolve your differences.

Marsha and I would like to invite you up to the house next weekend. This is a time when you need your friends. Let us know if you can make it; we would like very much to see you.

Best regards,

Will

Will

Reply to Sympathy/Condolence Messages

Just as it's important to acknowledge someone's loss, it's important to acknowledge the sympathy or condolence messages you receive in times of loss. If you are unable to respond yourself, have someone else write for you. The message would clarify this by beginning "Cheryl has asked me to thank you for . . . ," "Mother asked if I would thank you for . . . ," and so on.

Personal expressions of sympathy—such as flowers, assistance, contributions, support—that you receive should be answered with handwritten notes. In the case of funerals, cards accompanying flowers are collected and given to the family. This provides a list of people who should be thanked for their kindness and sympathy.

October 3, 19--

Dear Solveig and Dag,

Thank you for the many acts of kindness you did for me during the time of Frank's death. If it hadn't been for the caring and support of friends like yourselves, I don't think I would have made it through the funeral service and the days after.

I will never forget your kindness and love. Thank you.

Sincerely,

Louise

Louise

June 12, 19--

Dear José,

Lili asked me to thank you for the flowers you sent. They are gorgeous—we put them on the bedroom windowsill where Lili can see them first thing in the morning.

Your thoughtful gift arrived at the right time. Lili had been feeling very depressed about being sick so long. The flowers picked up her spirits considerably. Thank you so much.

Affectionately,

Marlene & Lili

Marlene and Lili

THANK-YOU'S

Thank-you notes are common courtesies extended to someone who has sent you a gift, provided hospitality, done you a favor, or extended other acts of kindness. Even if you thank the givers in person, at times a follow-up written note can let them know how deeply you appreciate their thoughtfulness.

Your thank-you notes should be handwritten on personal stationery or on commercial thank-you cards to which you add your own brief comments.

Send your messages promptly—within a day or two of the event or receipt of the gift. If you address your letter to one member of a family or a couple, include the others in the body of your message, "I'd like to thank you and Cliff . . . ," "Please thank your family as well. . . ."

Focus on the thank-you message and let it go at that. Save your news about job, family, or love life for your next letter.

Gifts

Gifts are probably the most common occasion for writing thank-you letters and notes. If you tend to put off such messages, keep a supply of attractive, pre-stamped postcards on hand. In that way, you make it easy for yourself to jot a message down on the card and send it off without having to search for stationery, envelopes, addresses, stamps, and pens.

Let the person know right away that the gift has arrived, even if you must write later to tell them how much you appreciated the gift.

Show real appreciation by describing what you like about the gift. If you received money, mention what you might spend it on. The idea is to make the giver feel that the choice was a good one and that you are pleased and delighted with the present.

If the gift is something you don't like or can't use, then simply thank the person for his or her thoughtfulness. Respect the giver even if you can't enjoy the gift.

December 28, 19--

Dear Aunt Ruby,

I <u>loved</u> the oil painting set you sent me! I have been wanting one like it for months and couldn't believe it when I unwrapped your present. I can't wait to try it out.

Thank you again — next time you come to visit I'll have oil paintings to show you!

Love,
Polly

June 23, 19--

Dear Mr. Mitsuyama,

Your graduation present was a wonderful surprise. Thank you so much for your congratulatory letter as well.

I plan on putting the money aside to help finance my first car. Since I've accepted a job with a suburban company, Tri-Arts Enterprises, I'll need a car to get back and forth to work.

Thank you very much for your generous gift. As a new graduate just starting out, I feel very supported by my family and friends.

Sincerely yours,

Jan Okamoto
Jan Okamoto

Belated Thanks for a Gift.   You received a gift four months ago and still haven't written a thank-you note. The more guilty you feel, the more you put it off. Yet there is a simple way to write belated thanks. Admit your error, and thank the person for the gift. Explain briefly why you didn't write before, and tell the giver what you have appreciated about the gift.

August 9, 19--

Dear Petula,

Please accept our belated thanks for the lovely cooking set you gave us for our wedding. Greg and I have been over-whelmed with setting up house and getting settled in new jobs. We apologize for the delay in acknowledging your thoughtful present.

We have used your pots and pans often. We just love them! They're such a pleasure to use that I've even convinced Greg to cook breakfast occasionally. They clean in no time, even when you-know-who (me!) burns something every now and then.

Thanks again, Petula, for your wonderful and useful gift.

Fondly,

Tabatha and Greg
Tabatha and Greg

Query About a Gift Sent but Not Acknowledged. When you send a gift but never receive a thank-you note or acknowledgment, you have a right to inquire about the reason. In most cases, the recipient has simply not gotten around to writing you, but gifts sent in the mail do get lost.

Give your recipient the benefit of the doubt in your letter of inquiry. Assume that the gift did not arrive or that some other reason has prevented the recipient from writing you. This leaves the door open for a belated thanks or a message that the gift never arrived. In either case you have obtained the information you want without harming your relationship.

October 2, 19--

Dear Opal,

I can't believe it's been six months since your wedding! You must be well settled into your new home by now.

Speaking of home, your cousin Glen and I have been con-cerned that you have not mentioned our wedding gift. We selected a set of towels and linens from Marshall Field's and asked that the package be delivered to your apartment.

If you never received it, please let us know so we can have the package traced. I would hate for you to think that Glen and I didn't send you anything. Please tell us if the gift arrived safely or not. Congratulations again to Fredrick and best wishes to you both.

Love from your cousin,

Norma
Norma

Hospitality

Thank-you notes for hospitality extended to you are known as ''bread-and-butter'' letters. Even though you thanked your host and hostess before you left, courtesy requires that you follow up with a cordial note of thanks two or three days after returning home. Such letters give you a chance to add to your thanks or to mention anything you forgot to say as you were leaving.

June 25, 19--

Dear Mr. and Mrs. Yolander,

Larry and I really appreciated your putting us up for the night on such short notice. The rest made a big difference on our final day of driving through the mountains.

We enjoyed talking with you — Wendy has told us so much about you that we felt we had been introduced a long time ago. If you're ever in Denver, please know that you have a place to stay in our house. Thank you again for your warm hospitality.

Sincerely,
Evelyn and Larry

Favors

It's good to be able to turn to friends and relatives for favors in time of need. It's also a welcome touch to thank friends or relatives in writing for their kindness and efforts on your behalf. State specifically in your letter what you appreciate and how much it means to you. Let them know that you value them for themselves, not just for what they have done.

Watching Children.   Watching someone else's children can be a favor tinged with heroism. It is quite a responsibility to shoulder, and your letter of thanks should take this fact into consideration.

> November 12, 19--
>
> Dear Ellen and Gubby,
>
>   We appreciate so much your taking care of Scott, Debbie, and Dana while we were at the Chemical Society convention. I know it can be a shock to suddenly have three lively children in your household all at once.
>   You both made a big hit with the children. Dana wanted to know if we were going away again soon and, if so, could they stay at your house? I think you've been adopted by my children!
>   Scott and Debbie told me about the railroad museum you went to and all the muffins and carrot bread they helped you make. You are both wonderful second parents for the kids. We appreciate your patience and concern for them. Thank you from the bottom of our hearts.
>
> Love,
> *Felicia and Dwayne*
> Felicia and Dwayne

Taking Care of a Pet.   Although not as big a job as taking care of children, watching someone's pet is also a responsibility. Don't assume that it's a job without effort or inconvenience. Acknowledge the person's willingness to put himself or herself out for you in your letter of thanks.

February 13, 19--

Dear Pahruiz,

I arrived home to a happy, contented cat last night. Thanks a million for taking the time to come over and feed Mr. Jenkins and play with him. I appreciate not only your care with his food and litter box but the attention you gave him — even brushing his coat!

It makes a big difference; he's not as starved for my attention when I come back. If you ever need someone to take care of Quinn when you're gone, call on me. Thanks again for your loving care!

Love,
Greta

Being a Good Friend.   Friends can give you the most important favor of all—their love and concern during a difficult or trying time. These moments deserve recognition. Tell them how their sharing helped you or what you valued about their actions. They may not be aware that they did anything special.

January 9, 19--

Dear Michael,

Just a note to say how much I appreciate your listening to me the other day when I was really depressed about breaking up with Rosanne. After ten years, it's been really hard to say goodbye.

You have a real knack for listening and letting a guy talk himself out of his misery. It's great to have you as a friend — it would have been much tougher to get through the holidays without your help.

Eric

WEDDINGS   (See also Announcements, Engagement)

Few occasions are surrounded with as much ceremony and tradition as weddings. As the beginning of a new life for two people, you naturally want everything to go as planned. Invitations and announcements reflect the type and style of wedding to be held, from highly formal to a more casual get-together of immediate family and friends. The following basic guidelines should help you in preparing invitations and announcements for most weddings. If you need more information, consult any of the books or magazines available on the market that specialize in wedding traditions and etiquette.

1. *Invitations* request people to come to the ceremony. They are mailed at least one month before the wedding date to give people a chance to arrange their schedule to attend and purchase gifts.

   Announcements simply let people know the wedding took place. They are mailed on the day of the wedding or a day or two later. They are sent only to those who did not receive invitations or were unable to attend the wedding.

2. Engraved invitations are appropriate for both formal and informal weddings. If the wedding is very small or quiet, invitations can be made by telephone or personal note.

3. Engraved invitations contain two envelopes. One contains the invitation and reception card. This envelope is not sealed; only the name of the guest is written on the outside. The second envelope is for mailing. The complete name and address of the guest is written on the outside.

4. Traditionally, the bride's parents are responsible for mailing the invitations and announcements. If the parents are not living, the nearest relative or a close friend may assume this task. Some couples choose to send invitations or announcements themselves.

5. Parents separated may unite their names on the invitation if they wish. However, if the parents are divorced, the parent

with whom the bride has lived generally issues the invitations and announcements. If the parent has remarried, the new couple(s) should list their names on the invitations.

6. The year is not generally used on invitations, but if it is, it should be spelled out (*Nineteen hundred and ninety-one*). The year should appear on a wedding announcement, along with the city and state in which the wedding took place.

7. Spell out all numbers, dates, and street addresses on formal invitations and announcements.

8. For a traditional or religious wedding, use the phrase "request the honor of your presence." Home, club, or hotel wedding invitations and reception invitations should be phrased "request the pleasure of your company." If the reception is before one o'clock, it is called a *breakfast*. If it is after one o'clock, it is called a *reception*.

9. Generally only family and close friends are invited to the reception. You may want to order two sets of invitations, with and without reception cards.

Traditional or Religious Weddings

Traditional weddings are more formal affairs, and the invitations or announcements reflect this formality. The correct form for a ceremony held in a church follows:

Dr. Natalie and Mr. Terrence Hold
request the honor of your presence
at the marriage of their daughter
Ruth Ellen
on Saturday morning, the eighth of October
at two o'clock
First Baptist Church
Denver

Reception Card.   The reception card accompanying the invitation would look like this:

> Dr. Natalie and Mr. Terrence Holt
> request the pleasure of your company
> at a reception
> Saturday, the eighth of October
> at five o'clock
> Fifty-five Harrison Avenue
>
> Please respond
> 878-5565

If the reception is given at the home of a relative or friend, the invitation should still be issued in the bride's parents' name. A card for this type of reception would look like the following:

> Dr. Natalie and Mr. Terrence Holt
> request the pleasure of your company
> at the residence of
> Ms. Anne Bradley and Dr. Leontyne Maxwell
> Fourteen Culvert Place
> immediately following the ceremony
>
> Please respond
> Fifty-five Harrison Avenue

The reply should be sent to the bride's parents and not to the people hosting the reception.

Reception Invitation Only. For guests invited to the reception only and not the ceremony, the following invitations are appropriate:

Dr. Natalie and Mr. Terrence Holt
request the pleasure of your company
at the wedding reception of their daughter
Ruth Ellen
and Mr. Gary Schoen
on Saturday, the eighth of October
at five o'clock
Fifty-five Harrison Avenue

R.S.V.P.
Fifty-five Harrison Avenue

Wedding and Reception Invitation Combined. If all the guests are invited to both the ceremony and the reception, a combination invitation can be used.

Dr. Natalie and Mr. Terrence Holt
request the honor of your presence
at the marriage of their daughter
Ruth Ellen
to
Mr. Gary Schoen
on Saturday, the eighth of October
at one o'clock
First Baptist Church
Denver
and afterwards at a reception
at Fifty-five Harrison Avenue

Please respond to
Fifty-five Harrison Avenue

Home Weddings

An invitation to a religious or traditional wedding is generally only for the ceremony—one reason a separate reception card is enclosed. Invitations to a home wedding, however, are generally for both ceremony and reception, making a separate reception invitation unnecessary. You can use either ''pleasure of your company'' or ''honor of your presence'' on the card.

Mr. and Mrs. Petro St. John
request the pleasure of your company
at the marriage of their daughter
Maria Pilar
to
Mr. Julio Conseco
on Friday, the seventh of June
at three o'clock
Twenty-two forty Lakeview Avenue
Hammond, Indiana

The favor of a reply
is requested

If the ceremony takes place at a residence other than the home of the bride's parents, the invitation would read:

Mr. and Mrs. Petro St. John
request the pleasure of your company
at the marriage of their daughter
Maria Pilar
and
Mr. Julio Conseco
on Friday, the seventh of June
at three o'clock
at the residence of Mr. and Mrs. Carlos Ramirez
Twelve Twenty-two Logan Street
Hammond, Indiana

Special Circumstances for Wedding Invitations

Today, with family situations so varied, double weddings, second or third marriages, and other special circumstances are common. In response, invitation forms have evolved to cover these situations. (Announcements would follow the same format as the invitations, with the addition of the year to the date of the wedding.)

Second Marriage.   In a second marriage, if the woman is young, her parents or nearest relative may issue the invitation. The format is the same as for first weddings, only the full name of the bride is used if she has kept her ex-husband's name.

Mr. Robert C. Walsh and Ms. Jacqueline Ross
request the honor of your presence
at the marriage of their daughter
Patricia Alice Bonnatelli
to
Mr. Anthony DuSable
(rest of invitation follows)

If the bride is more mature, or if there is no one in the family to issue the invitations, she may send them out in the following form:

The honor of your presence is requested
at the marriage of
Mrs. Patricia Alice Bonnatelli
and
Mr. Anthony DuSable
(rest of invitation follows)

Notice that the name of the bride always comes first, even on invitations that the bride and groom issue themselves.

Stepparents.   When the bride's mother has been divorced or widowed and remarries, the bride may either adopt the stepfather's name or retain the name of her original father. In either case, the full name of the bride is used. Both parents may present their daughter in marriage or only the mother, as shown below.

Mr. and Mrs. Conrad Steinhoff
request the honor of your presence
at the marriage of their daughter
Georgina Ilene Farkas
(rest of invitation follows)

OR

Mr. and Mrs. Conrad Steinhoff
request the honor of your presence
at the marriage of
Mrs. Steinhoff's daughter
Georgina Ilene Farkas
(rest of invitation follows)

Only One Parent.   If the bride's mother or father has died or divorced and the other parent is not available to participate in the ceremony, the invitations would be issued as follows:

Mr. Warren Clark
requests the honor of your presence
at the marriage of his daughter
Carol Anne
(rest of invitation follows)

Wedding Announcements

Wedding announcements have all the pomp and dignity of the invitations. They are issued by whoever issued the invitations. Announcements are sent only to those you could not invite to the ceremony but wish to inform of the event.

The format for an announcement for a traditional or religious wedding is as follows:

Dr. Natalie and Mr. Terrence Holt
have the honor of announcing
the marriage of their daughter
Ruth Ellen
to
Mr. Gary Schoen
on Saturday, the eighth of October
Nineteen hundred and ninety-two
First Baptist Church
Denver, Colorado

Handwritten Invitations

When the wedding is small or informal, handwritten, personal notes can be sent to the guests in lieu of formal, engraved invitations. The invitations should clearly state the time, place, and date of the wedding and whether the guest is invited to a reception.

March 15, 19--

Dear Latoya,

After six months of trying to get everything coordinated, Stefan and I have set the date — Saturday, July fifteenth, at two o'clock. We are having a very small wedding at his uncle's house, Mr. Casimir C. Pollock, 2453 West Elm, Rosemont, Illinois.

Stefan and I are asking only our closest friends and relatives, and we want very much for you to be there with us. Please say you'll come, and join us afterwards for a reception to celebrate.

You have been wonderful to both of us, and it would mean a great deal to have your blessing on our wedding day.

Love,
Kathleen

Recalling or Canceling Wedding Invitations

A variety of circumstances may cancel a wedding—an accident, natural disaster, death in the family, or a change of heart by the bride or groom. If the change occurs close to the wedding date, guests should be notified by telephone or telegram. However, if there is time, formal cards should be mailed to all the guests. If the reason is other than a bride's or groom's change of heart, always give the reason for the cancellation on the card.

> Mr. and Mrs. Hiroshi Nakamura regret
> that owing to an injury to the groom
> they are obliged to recall the
> invitations to their daughter Kim's
> marriage on Friday, the twentieth of April.

When the bride or groom decides to call off the wedding, the card need not give the reason. A simple statement of fact is all that is needed.

> Mr. and Mrs. Hiroshi Nakamura announce that the marriage of
> their daughter Kim and Mr. Joseph Kaniwa will not take place.

Acknowledging Wedding Invitations

A prompt reply when requested is required for home, club, or hotel weddings so that the bride's family can plan for the number of guests that will attend. Reception cards should be returned in their separate envelopes and marked as to whether the recipient will or will not attend. Regrets should briefly state the reason for the refusal.

M. _Carolyn Lewis and Graham Lewis_

will _____

will not _✓___

be able to attend the reception.

I'm so sorry Gabriella — we leave for New Zealand the day before. We'll be thinking of you.
—Carolyn

No response is required to a wedding announcement, although you may want to send a congratulatory note or a gift.

CHAPTER

≡SIX

CONSUMER ACTION LETTERS

As a customer in a consumer-oriented society, you expect a certain standard of quality from the products and services you purchase. When you don't get that quality, you have the right to demand an adjustment or response from those supplying the product or service.

The letters in this chapter show you how to obtain information or to stand up for your rights in a wide variety of consumer situations. You also have a few public and private agencies on your side that you should become familiar with: Better Business Bureau, Chamber of

Commerce, the consumer action columnists working for many local and state newspapers, and various state and local consumer advocacy groups.

In addition, your public library can supply various resources for consumer aid. Publications such as *State Administrative Officials Classified by Function,* published by the Council of State Governments, list various regulatory agencies that oversee insurance, banking, consumer affairs, and other consumer-oriented areas. The U.S. Office of Consumer Affairs in Washington, DC, and the Consumer Information Center in Pueblo, CO 81009, telephone number 1-719-948-3334, can supply you with a host of federal, state, and local consumer groups, complete with whom to contact and their telephone numbers. Call or write these agencies for the latest information.

If you cannot settle a dispute with a company or service provider through telephone calls or a personal visit, the next step is to write a letter. Follow these guidelines for consumer action letters.

1. *Find out who has the authority to grant your requests or satisfy your complaints.* Call the company or service provider and find out the name of the person who can take care of your concern or complaint. If you have only a company name, the public library's reference section can help you find out the telephone number and address of nearly any company in the country, and even many of them overseas.

2. *Write promptly.* Write within two to three days of receiving inadequate merchandise or service. Don't wait several weeks, hoping the company or service provider will have a change of heart. In many cases, the law requires that you write within a specified amount of time—ten, thirty, or sixty days—after receiving the product or service. The longer you wait, the weaker your case becomes.

3. *Save all receipts, correspondence, records of payments, and the like.* Keep a file of every transaction you make with the company or service provider. The more documented proof you have on hand to support your claim, the stronger your case and the more likely you are to win an adjustment or refund. *Never send an original document along with your complaint letter.*

Always send copies and keep the originals in your files. Otherwise, your proof may mysteriously vanish.

4. *Find out what legal recourse you have.* Call a lawyer, check with the local police department, contact the Better Business Bureau, or ask other consumer experts for help. Know your legal rights and what action you can take, particularly if your first letter fails to get results.

5. *Be firm but tactful; assume that you can work out a settlement.* You gain nothing by berating or abusing the dealer or service provider. State your case clearly, using the chronological or cause-and-effect formats described in Chapter 3.

6. *State specifically what action you want the recipient to take.* Don't assume the recipient will know. Say what you want—a refund, a reorder, a cancellation. Remember the four questions your letter must answer, as discussed in Chapter 1.

7. *Be willing to negotiate, if appropriate.* You may be able to get only part of what you want. Be willing to negotiate a settlement.

8. *Go straight to top management if you don't get a satisfactory response from lower levels.* If the sales manager or superintendent does not give you the response you want, write to the president or chief executive officer of the company. Although he or she probably will not handle the matter personally, you will alert the individual to the fact that a customer is dissatisfied. That may be enough for you to get results.

9. *Finally, always keep copies of letters you send.* Don't rely on memory—it can be notoriously unreliable when it comes to remembering exactly what you said in a letter.

GENERAL PRODUCT AND SERVICE LETTERS

The letters in this section deal with everyday consumer situations that most people encounter at some time in their lives. Notice that the writers state in the first sentence or two why they are writing. They get immediately to the point and keep their letter focused on the issue and what they want. They also supply order or part numbers, invoice numbers, or other essential identifying information to make it easier for the recipients to respond to their specific requests.

Requesting Deposit Refund

You may have occasion to put a deposit on merchandise, a vacation package, or other item to hold it until you can pay the full amount. If you change your mind, you can request that the deposit be refunded to you.

However, before requesting the full amount, check with the merchant or read over the written contract (if one is issued) to see if the terms grant all or only a portion of the deposit returned. Some merchants and travel agents have a timetable in which a decreasing portion of the deposit is refunded the closer one gets to the final purchase date.

June 20, 19--

Donna Montevecchi
Ticket Supervisor
Isle Royale National Park
87 North Ripley Street
Houghton, MI 49931

Dear Ms. Montevecchi:

I am writing to request a refund of my deposit on two round-trip tickets on the boat from Houghton to Isle Royale. We were to depart July 10 for the island and return to Houghton on July 18. My husband and I have had to cancel our vacation plans due to an illness in the family.

I have paid a deposit fee of $20 per ticket, for a total of $40 (check #815). I understand that we are still entitled to a full refund ten days before the departure date.

Please send the refund to me at the address below. We are very sorry not to be able to go on this trip. We have had many enjoyable vacations on Isle Royale in the past. I hope that we will be able to return next year.

Sincerely,

Roberta Chiang

Roberta Chiang
475 Madison Avenue
New Haven, Wi 54228

Incompetent Repair or Maintenance Work

Poorly done work is not only infuriating—it can be dangerous. You may experience a serious inconvenience and expense to have the work done over again. When repair people have done a poor job, write for an adjustment immediately. The work may be covered under a warranty or guaranty and may be done free of charge. Also, if the repair people damaged your property, you are more likely to get reimbursement if you write promptly.

In the example below, the writer lists what he wants the company to do to rectify matters.

August 1, 19--

Mr. Andrew Ditsler
Property Manager
Parliament Apartments
P.O. Box 672
Oklahoma City, OK 73102-3241

Dear Mr. Ditsler:

I am writing to complain about the installation of the weather-stripping around my living room windows last week.

First, your workers installed metal strips around all four windows, rendering them completely impossible to open. In the summer heat, the rooms are like blast furnaces.

Second, I had no notice that the workers were coming and was not at home when they arrived. They let themselves in and knocked over plants and furniture to get to the windows. They also broke several glass ornaments hanging in the windows—in general leaving a trail of destruction from one window to the next.

To repair this situation, I would like the following:

1. Please remove the top metal strips on the windows so I can open them again.

2. Please reimburse me for the broken ornaments, valued at $30 apiece (copies of the receipts for these items are enclosed) for a total of $120.00.

3. In the future, please give me at least 24 hours' notice before sending repair people to my apartment. I can prepare for them and be home when they arrive.

I have been a renter in your complex for over ten years and always paid my rent on time. In light of my long history as a tenant, I trust we can come to a satisfactory agreement on this matter. Thank you.

Sincerely,

Daniel Aynehsazan

Daniel Aynehsazan

Defective Product

Like shoddy repair or maintenance work, defective products can be a hazard as well as an inconvenience. Write promptly to request a credit, refund, or replacement item. Include the model number of the item and details of when and where you purchased it. If you spoke with anyone in the company about the item, mention their names in your letter and the outcome of your conversation.

October 19, 19--

Ms. Louise Pinkowicz
Customer Relations
Midwest Merchandise, Inc.
P.O. Box 6197
Sioux Falls, SD 57117

Dear Ms. Pinkowicz:

On September 20, I purchased a Randix AM/FM clock radio and cassette player, manufacturer's number #RWC650, at the Midwest Merchandise store, 1242 Northwest Highway, in Hastings, South Dakota. I paid $110.23 for the radio, as shown on the enclosed copy of the receipt.

The radio worked well for two weeks and then quit for no apparent reason. Also, the volume on the cassette player kept going loud and soft.

The warranty on the radio states that if the radio is defective for any reason, I can return it and get a replacement within 60 days of purchase. I talked to Ms. Wiloma Esterhaus at the Midwest store where I bought the radio, and she told me I had to mail the item to you to get my replacement.

I am enclosing the broken radio in this package; please send me a new radio of the same model. Thank you for your assistance.

Sincerely,

Peter Y. Wei

Peter Y. Wei
894 Westchester Rd.
Hastings, SD 57224

Actions of Transit Drivers, Conductors

Many people in urban and rural America depend on mass transit drivers and conductors to get to and from work, shopping centers, or other locations. These individuals tend to be anonymous until they do something to irritate or impress riders.

If you have been treated unusually well or ill by transit personnel, write a letter to the district supervisor of your city or regional transportation authority. The reference librarian can help you to locate the name and address of the appropriate individual to write.

In your letter, mention the driver's or conductor's name or badge number (if known), the bus or train number, and the route, date, and time in which the incident happened. Although the model letter below is complimentary, a complaint letter would follow the same format.

March 15, 19--

Mr. Maxwell Daley
District Supervisor
Regional Transportation Authority
1011 South Holland
Kansas City, KS 66101

Dear Mr. Daley:

I would like to commend the actions of one of your north suburban bus drivers, Yolanda Huff, for her kindness to me last Thursday, March 8, when I was riding on her route.

I am 78 years old and suffer from high blood pressure. In visiting my doctor, I take the #212 bus, which goes from Davis Avenue to North Court Plaza in Prairie Village. About halfway there, I began to feel dizzy and asked the driver to let me off at a restaurant where I could call my daughter.

The next thing I knew I was lying on the floor of the bus, and Ms. Huff was wiping my forehead with a damp cloth and offering me a glass of water. I had fainted, and she had quickly pulled into the parking lot of a Baskin-Robbins store to call for help. She waited until the paramedics arrived to take me to the doctor's hospital.

In a time when many bus drivers ignore us older folks and even seem to enjoy making it hard for us to get up the steps, I was touched by Ms. Huff's solicitude. She may have been a minute or two late arriving at North Court Plaza, but she made a frightening experience a lot less so. I thank her, and I thank you for hiring such a caring, competent driver.

Sincerely,

Mr. Anwar Youkanha
Mr. Anwar Youkanha

Poor Service at Store

If a clerk or salesperson provides poor service, report it to the management. It is management's responsibility to see that employees represent their firm in the best possible manner. As a consumer, you have considerable power to change the way you are treated.

In your letter, use the chronological format, telling the person what happened and what you would like them to do about it.

March 26, 19--

Ms. Sarita Ordonez
The Jewelry Tree
1011 Ligonier Street
Whiteside, TX 78075

Dear Ms. Ordonez:

Whether you realize it or not, a clerk in your store, Joe Murdoch, is hurting your business. His rude, brusque manner is making this customer think twice about buying jewelry in your shop.

Last Wednesday I came into your store to purchase a ring. Although there were no other customers in the store, I had to ask Mr. Murdoch several times to wait on me. He was impatient as I made my selection, and when I picked out an opal pendant priced at $160, he said, "You realize that it's real, don't you?"

All in all, he conveyed the impression that he doubted my ability to pay for the purchase. Granted, I was dressed in a sweatsuit, but someone should tell Mr. Murdoch that clothes do not make the woman. I had just come from an aerobics class.

Please, Ms. Ordonez, either fire Mr. Murdoch or institute a mandatory employee training course in customer service. I regard your store as one of the best jewelry shops in town and would hate to see a rude employee hurt your business.

Regards,

Beverly Wyler

Beverly Wyler

Seeking Help from Consumer Advocates

There are times when you can't get results on your own. Rather than give up, seek help from consumer advocates whose resources and influence may get results for you. Find out from your city hall, public library, Better Business Bureau, or local newspaper consumer expert where to turn for help for your particular situation.

Be ready to support your case with documents, receipts, warranties, correspondence, or other evidence.

April 2, 19--

Felicia Kaplan
Community Action League
City Hall
Latrobe, PA 15650

Dear Ms. Kaplan:

I need your help. I built a house eight years ago using a prefab design supplied through Smitty's Cedar Homes. My sales contract (copy enclosed) included a 20-year guarantee on the roof shingles. For the past several months, shingles have been falling off, and now my roof has started leaking.

When I tried to contact Smitty's about the problem, I discovered they had gone out of business. Next I tried the manufacturer, Morgan Shingle Co., but they say the guarantee was provided by the builder, not by them (see letter attached). They also say a new roof would cost close to $3,500. The bank where I have my mortgage said there was nothing they could do.

I'm just about out of ideas. Is my 20-year shingle guarantee worth the paper it's printed on? Is there any way I can go after the assets of the defunct Smitty's to pay for a new roof? I would appreciate any advice you can give me—at all possible speed. It's starting to rain again.

Sincerely,

Mary Zalweski

Mary Zalweski
8443 Petrie Lane
Latrobe, PA 15650

CAR PROBLEMS

Nearly everyone who owns a car has had some problems with mechanics, dealers, or manufacturers. Most problems are handled on the local level and can be settled by a phone call or a personal visit to the dealer or auto repair shop in question.

However, for those instances when you cannot get your problem resolved on the local level, you may need to go up the auto company's management ladder to get results. Also, you can turn to several agencies and consumer advocacy groups for help.

General Manager of Auto Dealership

The place to begin is with the general manager of your auto dealership. This person is authorized to handle problems at local dealership levels. In your letter, spell out the details of your problem, what has been done so far (include copies of any receipts, work orders, and so forth), and what you want the general manager to do.

September 2, 19--

Mr. David Gergun
General Manager
Southern Motors
234 N. Western Ave.
Cleveland, OH 44115

Dear Mr. Gergun:

Two and a half months ago I purchased a Torrin 4-cylinder passenger car at Southern Motors. This car had been recommended to me because of its reliability, great mileage, and low upkeep.

So far, none of these claims has proved true. The first week after I bought the car, it started to backfire and jerk every time I accelerated in second gear. Gas mileage plummeted from 28 miles per gallon to 15 miles per gallon.

Over the next five weeks, I brought the car into your service department four times to get the problem fixed. Each time it cost me about $120 (see work orders attached). Each time the car would work fine for a day or two and then the backfiring and jerking would start up again.

When I brought the car back the third and fourth times and demanded that it be fixed, the service manager seemed to think that the problem was all in my head. I'm no expert at cars, but whatever the mechanics are doing about the problem isn't working. The attitude is that my car is a low-priority warranty problem that can wait until more important work is done. In the meantime, I'm still driving a low-mileage, backfiring Torrin that's slowly costing me enough money to have the engine replaced.

Please, Mr. Gergun, I need your help to get my car restored to proper working order. Please talk to your service manager about working on my car until the problem is solved. I look forward to hearing from you.

Sincerely,

Joanne Thorpe
Joanne Thorpe
1487 Springdale Road
Cleveland, OH 44126

If the general manager does not give you a satisfactory response, your next step may be to write the district office manager. Include copies of your letter to the general manager plus work orders and other pertinent documents. Ask that someone from the district office inspect the car or be present at the dealership when you bring the car in for repair.

Corporate Headquarters

If the district level management offers no relief, contact the corporate headquarters of the company. Write to the vice president in charge of the division that produced your car and carbon copy your letter to the president of the company. Send the letter by certified mail, and include an itemized list of all work orders, correspondence, and steps you took to try to get the problem fixed. If this step does not get results, your next step is to take the matter to the Better Business Bureau or other consumer affairs group.

October 12, 19--

Mr. Paul Fontillas
Vice President
Torrin Division
Southern Motors, Inc.
3472 Warren Blvd.
Detroit, MI 48210

Dear Mr. Fontillas:

If you ever wonder why more Americans are buying foreign cars, my story will tell you. If the problems I've had with my new Torrin are not resolved, it will be the last Southern Motors car I will ever buy.

The Torrin I purchased has not worked right from the first week I bought it in June of this year. The poor service I received at the local and district levels has compounded the problem. Both the dealer from whom I purchased the car and the district manager have turned a deaf ear to my appeals to get the car fixed. Enclosed is an itemized summary of this sad, expensive (for me) story. I've also attached copies of seven work orders and the results of these "repairs." As you'll see, on the last occasion, a member of the district manager's office was present, but did little more than agree with the mechanics that "something sure is wrong." The car is now burning oil for some reason no one can fathom.

I have wasted time, money, and a lot of effort on this car, Mr. Fontillas. At this point, I have just about given up on repairing the car. Unless you take prompt action to correct the car's defects or refund the purchase price in full, I will be forced to take legal action regarding your company's refusal to honor the warranty.

Sincerely,

Joanne Thorpe

Joanne Thorpe
1487 Springdale Road
Cleveland, OH 44126

cc: President and Chief Executive Officer
Enclosures

Filing Complaint with Consumer Advocacy Group

If you cannot get action at the corporate level, one of the best groups to turn to for help is the Better Business Bureau. You can call in the BBB at any point in the process.

Simply notify the Bureau of your problem. They will send you a form to fill out, asking you to describe the situation and indicate what adjustment you would like the company to make. Copies of the completed form are filed with the BBB and sent to the automotive dealer or corporate headquarters.

The Bureau can then mediate disputes or take the matter to arbitration. The arbitrator, selected and trained by the BBB, can render a decision that is binding on both parties.

Special BBB departments, other customer advocacy groups, and the customer relations departments or major auto manufacturers can also help mediate disputes between car owners and dealers. They include:

Automotive Consumer Action Program (AUTOCAP)
8400 Westpark Drive
McLean, VA 22102
(703) 821-7000
Third-party arbitration of disputes

BBB AUTO LINE
Council of Better Business Bureaus
1515 Wilson Boulevard
Arlington, VA 22290
(703) 276-0100
Third-party dispute resolution program for AMC, Audi,
    General Motors and its divisions, Honda, Jeep, Nissan,
    Peugeot, Porsche, Renault, SAAB, and Volkswagen

BBB National Consumer Arbitration Program
Council of Better Business Bureaus
1515 Wilson Boulevard
Arlington, VA 22290
(703) 276-0100

Chrysler Customer Arbitration Board
P.O. Box 1718
Detroit, MI 48288
(313) 956-5970

Ford Consumer Appeals Board
P.O. Box 1805
Dearborn, MI 48126
(313) 337-6950
(800) 241-8450 (outside Michigan)

November 24, 19--
Complaint # 23-5677

BBB National Consumer Arbitration Program
Council of Better Business Bureaus
1515 Wilson Boulevard
Arlington, VA 22209

Dear Staff:

Since I purchased my new Torrin in June of 19-- I have had
nothing but trouble with both the car and the Southern Motors
company. I filed a complaint with the Better Business Bureau,
and Art Kravits, your contact at the district office, set up a meeting with the general manager at my local Southern Motors dealership. We went through the whole list of complaints, but were
unable to reach a satisfactory adjustment.

They agreed that the car had been poorly manufactured but
refused to either replace the car or refund the purchase price. I
understand that Southern Motors is committed to arbitrate complaints through the BBB's program.

I would like this dispute to be arbitrated by BBB, and will abide
by the decision. I believe this is the only way to get this matter
settled. Send me the agreement form, and let me know the time
and place of the arbitration hearing.

Sincerely,

Joanne Thorpe
Joanne Thorpe
1487 Springdale Road
Cleveland, OH 44126

Safety Design Flaw

Ever since consumer advocate Ralph Nader first made the public aware of the safety hazards in automobiles, customers have been quick to point out design flaws. Auto companies are responsive to complaints about safety hazards from customers.

If you have a safety-related problem with your car, you can get quick results by writing the manufacturer's vice president of product development. Among other things, the manufacturers will usually order the car fixed free of charge, even if the warranty has run out.

February 9, 19--

Mr. Y. A. Sunn
Vice President, Product Development
Torrin Division
Southern Motors, Inc.
3472 Warren Blvd.
Detroit, MI 48210

Dear Mr. Sunn:

I want to inform you of a potentially hazardous flaw in my new Torrin, which I purchased last year in September. When it rains or snows and the brakes get wet, they tend to lock if the car is going over 10 miles an hour when I apply the brakes. If I pump the brakes, they will unlock, but not before I've executed some hair-raising skids.

I've taken the car to my Torrin dealer, but they said because of the car's design, they could not correct the problem without taking the entire brake system apart and redesigning it. He suggested that I pump the brakes, never apply steady, full pressure.

This is fine if I'm the only one driving the car, but I'm not. My wife and two teen-age daughters will also use the car, and I don't like the idea of them driving around with this hazardous brake situation. Can't something be done about the design to fix this?

Sincerely,

Carlton Forslund

Carlton Forslund

FINANCIAL SERVICES—BANKS AND CREDIT CARDS

Banking and credit cards are a multi-billion dollar industry in the United States. Many people have more than one bank account and two or more credit cards. Although most transactions occur smoothly, when a bank or credit card company does make a mistake, or when you need to make an adjustment to your account, writing a letter is the best way to handle the matter.

Most credit card installment agreements specify that all queries, complaints, or adjustments regarding your statement must be made in writing, usually 30 to 60 days after you receive the statement. Save all receipts and monthly statements so that you can document your spending record.

The letters in this section show you how to query errors and request adjustments. For more detailed help, two books offer excellent information. They are *Credit Card Secrets,* edited by Howard Strong, The Boswell Corporation, P.O. Box 7100, Beverly Hills, CA 90212-7100, and *The Credit Power Handbook for American Consumers,* by Daniel K. Berman, published by Credit Power Publishing Company, 44 Montgomery Street, 5th Floor, San Francisco, CA 94104.

You can also appeal to the Better Business Bureau and consumer advocacy groups specializing in consumer credit. Consult your public library or city hall to find out whom to contact.

Error on Bank Statement

In many cases, you can settle an error on your bank account statement by taking the statement to the bank's customer service department and having them look into the matter. When this solution doesn't produce results, however, write a letter to the customer service manager or vice president of the bank, stating the error and what action you want taken. Always keep a copy of your correspondence and include the number of your account.

May 14, 19--
Account No. 000745-23-7554

Mr. Emilio Chavez
Customer Services Manager
Home State Bank
5419 Davis Street
Tuscon, AZ 85712

Dear Mr. Chavez:

I would like to point out an error on my May bank statement that was supposed to be corrected but was not. In April, the bank mistakenly transferred $800 from my business account to my personal checking account. This left my business account short, and several checks bounced.

When I pointed out the error to your customer service department, they assured me I would not be charged a service fee for the returned checks. They also promised to cover any more checks presented for payment on that account.

However, I find on my May statement that not only was I charged a service fee for each returned check, but two more checks were returned for insufficient funds at the end of April. This whole matter has caused me some embarrassment with suppliers, and I would like you to straighten out the matter.

Please cover any more checks presented for payment on my account, and remove the service charges. I am happy to pay for my mistakes, but I don't relish paying for mistakes the bank makes. Thank you for your assistance.

Sincerely,

Nola Hewitt-Kramer

Nola Hewitt-Kramer, President
JACKET DESIGNS, INC.

Credit Card Billing Error

Billing errors on credit card statements cover a wide range of situations. The Federal Fair Credit Billing Act, passed to protect consumers, lists the following as "errors."

1. The statement lists a charge for something you didn't buy.

2. It lists a charge you cannot understand.

3. It lists a charge for something you found unacceptable, whether a service or a product, and returned or refused.

4. It does not show credit for payments made or goods returned.

5. It shows a mistake in calculating interest, monthly payments, principal, or other figures.

6. It was not mailed to your correct address (you must let the company know at least 20 days before the billing date of a change in address).

7. It shows anything that looks wrong to you. According to the law, if you state *in writing* that something is a "billing error," the credit card company must treat it as a billing error.

In writing the company to correct the statement, follow three basic steps: (1) Include your account number, name, address, and date you wrote the letter; (2) use the phrase "billing error" in your letter; (3) state the reason for the billing error; and (4) include copies of your statement and any receipts, proof of purchase, or other documents. *Do not send originals.*

February 3, 19--
Account No. 5412-346-56623

Ms. Lucy Van Dorn
BankCard of America
Customer Service
245 Appletree Road
Wilmington, DE 19824

Dear Ms. Van Dorn:

I am writing to report a billing error on my December and January credit card statements. According to the December statement (see copy attached), I was charged $345.00 for a TV purchased from Talco Electronics. I returned the TV and requested a credit to my account for $345.00 (see letter attached).

Yet on my January statement, the same charge has appeared again, this time with a late fee attached because your computer claims I underpaid the minimum monthly amount due. I have telephoned your customer service department, and they have no record of any letter I sent requesting that $345.00 be credited to my account.

Would you please correct this error? I have enclosed the receipt from Talco Electronics, which shows that I returned the TV and that a credit voucher was sent to your company. I appreciate your assistance in this matter.

Sincerely,

Arthur Lee Kang

Arthur Lee Kang
3482 North Plaza Road
Wilmette, IL 60091

Stop Payment on Credit Purchase

Few people know that if you pay for a product or service by credit card and then find the item or service unsatisfactory, you can stop payment by notifying the credit card company immediately.

June 10, 19--
Account No. 5217-445-8876

Chemical Bank of Connecticut
Mastercard Division
245 West Holloway
Hartford, CT 06112

Dear Ms. Lacey:

As I mentioned on the phone, I wish to correct a billing error on my statement by stopping payment for National Magazines, Inc. I had originally ordered several magazines from this company, and agreed to pay the total bill in four quarterly installments of $49.95 every three months beginning in April. A copy of the contract is enclosed.

I find instead on my May statement that the company has already charged three of these installment payments, running up my total bill to $149.85. The whole purpose of arranging installment payments was to spread out the cost of the magazines. Apparently this company doesn't believe in abiding by a signed agreement.

Therefore, I wish to stop any further payment to National Magazines and would like a refund of the amount already charged to my account. Please make the adjustment to my bill. I will be happy to pay the other charges. Thank you.

Sincerely,

Njoki Assan-Namawar

Njoki Assan-Namawar
2214 Maple Ave.
Crystal Lake, IL 60014

HOME—APARTMENT, CONDOMINIUM, HOUSE

This section presents model letters covering some of the more common situations facing renters and owners—from moving into a new home to requesting repairs to asking for a reassessment on real estate taxes.

Moving

Moving can be an unpleasant experience. Yet there are steps you can take to make the transition from one home to another a little easier.

Many moving companies offer pamphlets on how to organize a move. The U.S. government also can offer some help. The Interstate Commerce Commission provides information on how to organize an interstate move. Write to the National Consumer Assistance Center, Interstate Commerce Commission, Washington, DC, 20423.

Missing or Damaged Item Claim.   Even the best moving company can make mistakes. If an item of yours is damaged or lost, you can obtain reimbursement for the item if your moving contract so states. In your letter, include your order number and all details of your claim. Be sure to have proof of the value of your item—either a receipt for its purchase, an expert's assessment of the item, or other evidence.

September 3, 19--

Leonard Lynch, Agent
Axle Van Lines, Inc.
500 North State Street
Chicago, IL 60610

Dear Mr. Lynch:

I am writing to notify you of a claim for damaged goods against your company. On August 24, I moved from Chicago to Pittsburgh, Pennsylvania. The assessed weight of the move was 3,000 pounds, and my order number was 1234-56.

The move went smoothly, but on opening the housewares box that your movers had packed, I discovered that my great-grandmother's cut-glass punch bowl had been shattered beyond repair. The bowl is literally irreplaceable, not only because of its sentimental value but because manufacturers no longer make cut glass like that anymore. I have, however, priced the nearest facsimiles of cut-glass bowls like my great-grandmother's. Enclosed is a list of prices at various stores; the average, you'll see, is $800.

My contract states that the liability insurance I purchased covers losses of up to $2,500. I would like you to reimburse me for the damaged bowl. Please send me a check at the above address in the amount of $800. It is too bad this unfortunate accident occurred. Otherwise, I was very pleased with your service.

Sincerely,

Anne Marie Stawinski

Anne Marie Stawinski

Notifying Others of a Change in Address. Although the change-of-address form at the post office will take care of forwarding your mail, you should notify credit card companies, utilities, and others of your new address. This is particularly important if services must be shut off or turned on. In your letter to a utility, be sure to mention how the service representatives can get into the apartment or house if you are not available to let them in yourself.

May 24, 19--
Account #1-01-23-5532

Customer Service
Northern Illinois Gas Co.
P.O. Box 2020
Aurora, IL 60507-2020

Dear Customer Service:

Please have the gas in my new home turned on by June 15. I will
be moving to 735 Madison Street in Evanston on June 14. You
can obtain the key to the house from Lynda Davis Realtors (708-
555-1367).

The house contains a gas-operated stove, wall oven, furnace,
and water heater. Thank you for your assistance.

Sincerely,

Jamil Hassain
Jamil Hassain

Apartment

You may need to write to management in order to recover your security deposit, request repairs or maintenance, complain about noisy or
messy neighbors, arrange for rental payments, or to sublet or break a
lease. These model letters show how to approach management, or if
you are the management, how to approach renters.

Obtaining Security Deposit.   Ordinarily, the security deposit is
returned within a short time after you move out of an apartment
building. In cases where the manager or owner is reluctant to return
your deposit, a letter requesting it is appropriate. If your requests do
not get results, your next step is to consult a lawyer.

The law is clear: Owners or managers must return tenants' security deposits, provided the money has not been used to repair damage
to the premises inflicted by the tenant. You have recourse to Small

Claims court if your own efforts do not get results. In many instances, you can file a claim without needing a lawyer. Check your lease to determine how long the management or owner has to return your deposit.

September 30, 19--

James Brown
Property Manager
Windham Apartments
P.O. Box 733
Carlsbad, KY 42030

Dear Mr. Brown:

This certified letter reiterates my request that you return my security deposit of $700 on my 1500 Maple Street apartment. My lease expired June 30, and I moved to my new address 2022 Fairmont Street.

After being a tenant for eight years, I left the apartment in better condition than I found it, putting up shelves and installing grounded wiring and sockets, which you approved.

I'm sure you're aware that you are required by law to refund my security deposit within 45 days of my departure. It has now been three months, and I've written you three letters. If I do not have your check for $700 in hand by October 7, I will have to refer the matter to my attorney. If that happens, you have to pay twice the amount of the deposit as well as attorney and court costs.

Save yourself the expense. Please refund my security deposit within seven days.

Regards,

Alicia Torres

Alicia Torres
2022 Fairmont Street
Carlsbad, KY 42030

Noisy/Messy Fellow Tenants.   Apartment dwellers are particularly vulnerable to their neighbors. When one of your neighbors is messy or noisy, and you cannot resolve the matter with a friendly talk, write to the managers or owners of the building. It is their responsibility to see that tenants observe the rights of others.

If you are a long-time tenant, mention this fact. If the neighbors are violating local zoning or other ordinances, mention this as well. Notice of violations, with their potential for city intervention, will provide an added incentive to the owner to take action.

November 13, 19--

Pauline Mitchell, Owner
Hudson Apartments
P.O. Box 332
Sioux City, IA 51123

Dear Ms. Mitchell:

I live in your 256 Davis/Elmwood building, apartment #354. As I write this letter, the din from my upstairs neighbors is all but drowning out the sound of the typewriter. You must be aware that the Choms (apt. 454) have six children, all under the age of 12, in a one-bedroom apartment.

I have been a tenant in your building for six years now, and have never had cause to complain about my neighbors before. But the kind of commotion in the Chom apartment disrupts the lives of everyone who lives below, above, or to either side of them. The noise is virtually constant from six in the morning to ten or eleven at night. The children run up and down the hallways at all hours, use the wheelchair ramp as a playground, and jump so hard on their floors that the plaster is flaking off my ceiling. More seriously, the crowding of eight people in a one-bedroom apartment violates our local zoning laws.

I am not against children in apartment buildings, just against packing so many of them into one small space. If you cannot arrange other accommodations for this family, I shall be forced to report you to the local zoning board. Other tenants I have talked to are also willing to take this step. Please see what you can do to rectify this situation and let the rest of us get some sleep. Thank you.

Sincerely,

Ashoka Nalamwar

Requesting Repairs.   Tenants who are handy can do minor repairs in an apartment, but most repairs should be handled by the management. Check your lease to see what recourse you have if the management is reluctant or slow to respond to your requests. Tenants' organizations, city inspectors and officials, and other city or citizen action groups may be able to intervene on your behalf if necessary.

May 2, 19--

Robert DeSable
Manager
Ridge/Maple Apartments
336 South Everest
San Francisco, CA 94122

Dear Mr. DeSable:

Two weeks ago I asked if you would take care of two maintenance problems in my apartment: a broken refrigerator and a leaking radiator in my neighbor's upstairs apartment. So far neither repair has been made, and the problems are getting worse.

There is not enough insulation between the refrigerator compartment and the freezer. Either I keep the freezer at the proper temperature and everything else in the refrigerator also freezes, or I keep the refrigerator at the right temperature and everything in the freezer melts. If the refrigerator cannot be repaired, it should be replaced. Anything less would be a violation of city health ordinances.

The other problem, the neighbor's leaking radiator, is now so bad that my living room ceiling is cracking and bubbling, and water sometimes drips down my wall. If this is not repaired immediately, you will have an even more expensive job on your hands in the near future.

I have spoken with the city inspector, who says that both these items are clear violations of city ordinances for maintaining apartment dwellings. He asked me to let him know if and when you have made the necessary repairs. I would like very much to tell him next week that they have been taken care of. Please have someone come over and see to the refrigerator and radiator. Thank you.

Regards,

Arlene Ritter

Arlene Ritter

Breaking a Lease. You may find it necessary to break a lease before the full term is up. You may be transferred to a new job, find a better place, or need to respond to a family emergency. Many leases contain provisions that require the current tenant to find someone to sublet, or take over, the lease. Others state that the tenant will be charged a fee to have the management take on this responsibility.

Regardless of what the lease states, your chances of amicably breaking the lease increase if you have someone you can recommend to take over your apartment. You want to leave under friendly circumstances if possible, because you may want to use the building owner or manager as a reference in the future.

May 2, 19--

Robert DeSable, Manager
Ridge/Maple Apartments Management
336 South Everest
San Francisco, CA 94122

Dear Mr. DeSable:

I am currently a tenant in the Ridge apartments on Market Street. I am writing to ask if it would be possible to end my lease, which runs to October 1 of this year, four months early. When I signed the one-year lease, I did not know that I would be offered a job in Portland that has proven too tempting to refuse.

I know my lease does not have any provision for subletting, but I have two proposals and hope that you'll find one of them satisfactory. First, I could vacate the apartment by May 31 and pay an extra month's rent of $800. This would provide rental income for one month during which you could renovate the apartment for the next tenant.

Second, I have a friend who is very interested in subletting my apartment as is, for the same rent, until the lease runs out. She would probably renew for the next year. She has great references and a solid job at Bank of America.

Please let me know if either of these proposals is acceptable to you. I need to make this move by the end of May, but couldn't afford to pay two rents, one here and one in Portland, for the next six months. I hope we can work something out to our mutual benefit.

Cordially,

Kerry Knobeldorff

Kerry Knobeldorff
Apartment #214

Arranging for Late Rent Payment.   Occasionally renters find themselves short of funds and unable to make rent payments on time. If this happens to you, notify the management at once either by telephone or by letter. Don't simply say you can't make the payment. Explain the circumstances and offer a solution—you will pay at such-and-such a time, you will pay part of the rent and the rest at a later date in the month, and so on. Remind the management of your past record of prompt payments and mention that once your cash flow problem is solved, the rent will be paid on time as usual.

January 28, 19--

Tonia Farrell, Owner
TCF Properties
4423 Hazel Street
Chicago, IL 60626

Dear Ms. Farrell:

I am currently a tenant in your Tower Street apartments, and am writing to ask for an extension on time allowed to pay my February rent. According to my lease, rent is due no later than the 5th of each month. Unfortunately, I will be short of funds in February and will need to have an extension on the due date to February 20th.

My company, Laurel Publishing, was purchased December 2 by a New York firm, which moved the entire operation to New York. Those of us who were laid off were awarded severance pay, but we have not received it. The lawyers promise us that the payments will arrive by February 15.

I have been a tenant in your building for six years and have never missed a rent payment. I love the apartment and want very much to stay. If you will grant me a two-week extension on February's rent, I'm sure my finances will be back on track before the March rent is due. I will be starting another job on March 1. Thank you for your consideration.

Sincerely,

Conrad Klaven

Conrad Klaven
Apartment 3E

Getting Overdue Rent.   Sometime you may find yourself trying to collect a late rental payment. Assume that the individual will pay. However, be firm about the consequences if your request is not met. In most cities, tenants must be several months behind on rent payments before they can be evicted. Even then, you must go through the expense and bother of finding another tenant. Thus, it is to your advantage if you can work out a solution with the current tenant.

March 15, 19--

Mr. Conrad Klaven
Apartment #3E
1515 Tower Street
Chicago, IL 60646

Dear Mr. Klaven:

Over a month ago you wrote and asked for an extension on the due date for your February rent. You stated you would pay the rent by the 20th and make the March payment on time. To date we have not received either the late February payment or your March rent.

We attempt to be understanding when tenants have lost their jobs or are short of cash for reasons beyond their control. However, you have not kept your side of the agreement, and we are concerned about your ability to continue paying the rent for the remainder of the year.

Mr. Klaven, do not jeopardize your fine record with our management. Please contact me at the number below to discuss how we can work out this problem. If we do not hear from you in three (3) days, we will be forced to take legal action. Please let us know either when we can expect payment or how you intend to arrange to pay for the rent you owe.

Very truly yours,

Tonia Farrell

Tonia Farrell
261-5592

Condominium

The responsibilities of condominium ownership are shared by the owners who belong to a board or association. This body sets the policies for the units and establishes assessment fees for maintenance and any repairs or extra expenses.

Letters you are likely to write as a condominium owner will generally be to the board, or as a member of the board to other owners.

Monthly Assessments. Condominium unit owners pay monthly assessments for maintenance and repairs. The condominium board or association assesses the amount and informs unit owners of any changes. If you must write a letter telling owners of an increase in monthly assessment fees, use the diamond sequence, giving reasons before stating the amount of the increase.

May 12, 19--

(Individual Unit Owner's name)
9255 Bonnard Drive
Gaithersburg, MD 20878

Dear Member,

As you know, this past winter has been particularly hard on our community. We have had to replace the central heating unit and the hot water heater, an expense which totaled $12,000. This amount has depleted our cash reserve. Yet Rockville Park has always prided itself on high maintenance standards and grounds upkeep.

If we are to maintain these standards, we must increase our operating budget by raising each owner's monthly assessment from $100 to $200. With summer fast approaching, we all know the pool will need repair and the common areas will require renovation.

We feel sure you will agree this is a necessary step in maintaining our joint and individual property values. Please try to attend the special meeting on Wednesday, May 18, at 8:00 PM in the workout room.

The enclosed proposal details the repairs and maintenance we would like to have done. Please read it over and come prepared to discuss this issue. This is your association, and we want to know what you think.

Sincerely,

Rockville Park Board of Directors

To protest an assessment increase you would follow the inverted pyramid format, stating your protest in the first sentence or paragraph, then following with your reasons. Either present the most important reason first, or save it until last. Your protest may have more impact if you can come up with an alternative plan or proposal.

May 14, 19--

Board of Directors
Rockville Park Condominium Association
9255 Bonnard Drive
Gaithersburg, MD 20878

Dear Directors:

I just received your letter notifying me that you plan to increase my monthly assessment from $100 to $200. If you want to know what I think, I say—wait a minute!

An increase of 100% seems excessive to me, particularly since I do not agree that we have the "highest maintenance standards." I paid extra for a southern unit with a view of the hills, yet last fall that view was marred by a huge mound of leaves. After waiting almost a month for the maintenance staff to bag them for disposal, I finally spent a Saturday afternoon doing it myself.

In addition, I've waited weeks for the maintenance people to adjust the water pressure in my bathroom, to fix the laundry machines, and to have my unit repainted. Each time I call I'm told that "It's not a high priority." If maintaining units is not a high priority, what is?

In light of these and other shortcomings, I believe the 100% increase is excessive. I've discussed this with a number of other unit owners and they all agree. We would like to hold an association meeting to discuss this issue on May 15 at 8:00 p.m. in my home. Please let me know how many directors can attend.

Sincerely,

Edmund Koleff-May

Edmund Koleff-May
Unit #128

House

Some of the more common complaints of homeowners involve dealing with building contractors and handling real-estate tax assessments. Although most contractors are reputable and deliver what they promise, when you get stung by one who doesn't, it's time for a letter to straighten matters out. In the examples below, one letter is to a contractor about a particular piece of work, the other is to a builder constructing a new home.

Letter to Contractor.   If a contractor provides poor service or materials, write a letter to the individual or firm. State your complaint and what you would like done. Be prepared to back up your letter with documentation.

August 30, 19--

Warren Momcek, President
Ideal Fence Co.
1300 Bluegrass Road
Nashville, TN 72609

Dear Mr. Momcek,

I am sending this letter by registered mail because I have been unable to contact you via telephone. On June 3 you contracted to build me a six-foot-high cedar fence, with an additional four feet of stake underground. The completion date was July 1, and the agreed price was $800. (A copy of the contract is attached.)

My quarrel is not that you didn't start the fence until July 1, or that the construction ran $300 over the agreed price. I am objecting to the fact that I have since discovered the fence extends only two feet underground, not the four feet required by village code, and that it was built with wood untreated for outdoor use.

I would like you to refund the $300 I paid over the agreed price, which is what it will cost to have the wooden fence treated and restaked. If I do not receive a check in that amount by September 5, I will turn the matter over to my attorney and report your company to the Better Business Bureau. It will be far costlier if you were ordered to replace the fence or refund all my money.

Regards,

Aretha Hubbleworth

Aretha Hubbleworth

Real-Estate Taxes. Many home owners find their real-estate taxes increasing steadily from year to year. If you feel your home has been unfairly assessed compared to your neighbors', you can protest the assessment and ask for an adjustment. Back up your claim by showing the assessed value of neighboring homes of comparable size, age, construction, and property to yours. These figures are generally printed in the local newspaper when assessments are mailed to home owners. Although paying taxes may be inevitable, you may be able to change the amount you have to pay.

May 1, 19--

Teresa Trebelhorn
Tax Assessor for Donagel Township
156 Ober Drive
Donegal, PA 15653

Dear Ms. Trebelhorn:

I have just received notice that my home's valuation has more than doubled! Last year my property taxes were $1800; this year the bill is $3800. Since I have not made any improvements or additions to my house or land, and the neighborhood is not appreciating, I am at a loss to understand such an increase.

If this figure is not a clerical error, let me buttress my case with some pertinent facts. I quote from the list of assessed valuation published in the Donegal Echo today. My home is listed first, then three of my neighbors'. All our homes are three-bedroom, one-car garage construction on about a half acre of land.

Owner	Address	Assessed Value	
		Land	Building
Summerhill	1725 Elm Ave.	$3,000	$67,000
Slivak	1742 Elm Ave.	1,500	38,000
Luther	1902 Chestnut St.	1,700	42,000
Chiang	1906 Chestnut St.	1,350	36,000

As you can see, the valuations of the other three homes are similar, yet my home is valued at roughly twice the price.

I could give more examples, but the point is that I believe my home has been overvalued and unfairly assessed. Please send the appraiser to reinspect the structure or provide me with an explanation for my higher tax rate. Thank you for your assistance.

Sincerely,

S. G. Summerhill

S. G. Summerhill
1725 Elm Ave.
Index No. 765-890-2

INSURANCE

Every insurance company is characterized by a blizzard of paper-work—files, claims, notices, policies, and on and on. The rule of thumb here is *write, don't call* when you need to correspond with your insurance company. Your written letters will be added to your file and serve as documentation. If possible, work through your insurance agent, who can often cut through red tape and speak out for you if you have trouble getting what you want from the company. Always note your policy number on any correspondence.

Should you need help in adjusting or mediating a claim or dispute, each state has an insurance department or division that licenses and regulates insurance agents and companies operating out of that state. You can find out who to contact in the publication *State Administrative Officials Classified by Function,* available in the public library reference section. Or you can write to the following agencies:

American Council of Life Insurance/Health Insurance Association of America
1001 Pennsylvania Avenue NW
Washington, DC 20004
Association of life, accident, and health insurance companies doing business in the United States

Insurance Information Institute
110 William Street
New York, NY 10038
(212) 669-9200
(800) 221-4954 (toll free outside New York)

Changing Policy

Making a change in your policy can be as simple as adding a beneficiary to your life insurance or as complex as requesting that new drivers be added to your auto insurance and your collision coverage be increased.

You can make the change either by writing to your insurance agent or directly to the company. Be sure to state clearly what changes you would like.

October 13, 19--
Policy No. GL-12-4599

Mutual Insurance Company
53 Madison Avenue
New York, NY 10010

Dear Staff:

I would like to change my accident insurance policy to Plan B in your schedule. This would decrease my monthly premium payments to $85.00 and increase my deductible to $300.00. I understand that Plan B includes outpatient surgery and dental expenses, similar to Plan A.

Please make this change effective immediately and send me a new policy as soon as possible. Thank you.

Sincerely,

Daniel Karbala

Daniel Karbala

Providing Claim Information

When you need to file an insurance claim, you generally fill out a form and supply a description of the incident—accident, illness, theft, and so on. Be as complete as possible, listing stolen items, for example, or any treatments not mentioned on the insurance claim form that may be covered by your insurance.

May 25, 19--
Policy No. #18-994-2344

Roberta Wong-Brink, Agent
Mutual Insurance Company
2450 Ridge Road
Kansas City, MO 64115

Dear Ms. Wong-Brink:

You asked for a list of items that were damaged in the flood last week. We have finally sorted out our belongings and put together a complete list.

Item	Price	Purchased
One hide-a-bed sofa	$650	12/1/90
Three wicker chairs	345	11/3/87
One Persian rug	985	3/22/88
One 19″ color TV	356	Summer 86
One Sony VCR	214	Fall 88

Luckily the other rooms were not affected. Our den was the only room below ground level, and the river just poured through the windows. We had about three feet of water in the room.

Our homeowners insurance should cover the losses we suffered. I believe we took out the rider on flood insurance at your suggestion about two years ago. I must say we regard you as something of a prophet now. Thanks for helping us settle this matter.

Sincerely,

Angelo Parrish

Angelo Parrish

Cashing In or Requesting Payment on Policy

At times you may want to cash in an insurance policy or annuity or request a payment when you are the beneficiary of someone else's policy. Your agent can make the request for you or you can write directly to the company.

November 3, 19--   Policy No. AE45-566-7832

Mutual Life Insurance
53 Madison Avenue
New York, NY 10010

Dear Staff:

I am enclosing the completed and signed claim form and a copy of my wife's death certificate, as you requested. Mrs. Dinkins' legal address at the time of her death was 3415 East Monroe, Tacoma, WA 98412.

Please pay the settlement in one lump sum. Since there are considerable medical expenses left unpaid, I would appreciate a settlement as soon as possible. Thank you.

Sincerely,

Stephen Dinkins

Stephen Dinkins

Appealing Nonrenewal Notice

Insurance companies base their decisions on whom to insure on the law of averages and the law of large numbers. This means that when a certain number of claims have been filed within a particular area or age group, the company may classify that area or group as high-risk. The company generally terminates insurance for everyone in that area or group, regardless of their individual records. Policyholders are informed through written notices that their insurance will not be renewed.

If such a termination happens to you, you can appeal the decision either directly to the company president or to the state regulatory agency. Be prepared to show evidence of your good record and the number of claims you have actually filed.

July 6, 19--
Policy No. 774-56-8993

Ms. Cynthia B. Lewis
President
Mutual Insurance Company
53 Madison
New York, NY 10010

Dear Ms. Lewis:

I am writing to protest the arbitrary cancellation of my health insurance policy by Mutual Insurance Company. On June 24 I received notice from your company that my major medical insurance policy would not be renewed. The reason was listed as "unusually high number of claims."

I learned from my agent that the company has classified my age group (55–60) as a high-risk group and has arbitrarily terminated insurance for everyone in that group. In the ten years I have had my policy, I have made only two claims, both for minor outpatient surgery. Otherwise, I have remained in excellent health.

I believe that rather than cancelling insurance across the board, Mutual Insurance should review individual policy holders to determine which ones are not making an excessive number of claims. Over the past ten years, I have always paid my premiums promptly, and never filed for any treatments that were not legitimately covered by the policy.

At my age, getting new insurance at the same price will be difficult. I am sure that once the facts in my case are made clear, you will renew my policy on the present terms.

Sincerely,

Mrs. Bertha Whitsun-Pitts

Mrs. Bertha Whitsun-Pitts
1800 Fortuna Drive
Frankfort, KY 40612

Speeding Up Settlement

You've filed a claim, provided all pertinent information as required by the company, and waited . . . and waited for your reimbursement check. If your repeated requests for settlement of your claim get nowhere, you can turn to the state insurance commission for help. State the facts of your case briefly, mentioning what efforts you made to settle the matter with the company.

February 24, 19--

Mr. Roger C. Highwater
Commissioner
Department of Insurance
Public Protection and Regulation Cabinet
229 W. Main St.
Frankfort, KY 40601

Dear Mr. Highwater:

I need your help in speeding up the payment of a claim I filed with Mutual Insurance Company nearly four months ago (my policy number is 43-5667-892). They have repeatedly delayed what should have been a routine settlement.

Last August I injured my lower back in a fall at my home. I was treated at Clear Oaks Community Hospital and underwent two months of physical therapy and manipulative treatment under the care of Dr. Helen Voorhees. I paid all doctor bills, hospital, x-ray, physical therapy, and laboratory bills out of my own pocket. The total cost amounted to $1250.00.

Mutual's claim department said I should wait and submit all medical expenses at one time. I did so on October 3. It has now been four months since I filed my claim, and I have yet to see any money from Mutual. When I called their claim department, a Mr. Saginaw said it was a computer error. I called again, and this time someone lost my claim. The third time I called, they had found the claim but were experiencing some delays in processing it.

By now I am running out of patience. I fulfilled all of Mutual's requirements and should be reimbursed for my expenses. Can you contact the company and speed up the process? Maybe they need to hear from an outside authority.

Thank you,

Phyllis R. Stein

Inadequate Settlement

You may find at some point that even though a claim is settled promptly, the amount is inadequate to cover your losses. The first step is to write to the insurance company for an adjustment. Let them know that if they are unwilling to respond to your claim, you will take the matter to court. If the amount is under $1,000, Small Claims court can often settle the matter relatively quickly. If your case is sound, the insurance company will have to pay court costs as well as your claim.

April 26, 19--

Mr. V. I. Tyson
Claims Manager
Mutual Insurance Company
53 Madison Avenue
New York, NY 10010

Dear Mr. Tyson:

Enclosed please find the check that you issued to me for repairs to my front porch caused when Harris Pothus, your insured, struck the porch with his van.

The $450 that your adjustor determined was fair compensation is considerably below the actual cost to repair my porch. I had three written estimates (enclosed) from three reputable contractors. The lowest estimate was $675. If you attempt to settle for less than this amount, I will take the matter to Small Claims Court. We will let the court recover the cost of the repairs.

Please send a revised settlement check by May 5, or I will instruct my lawyer to start court action.

Yours truly,

Gail Houser

Gail Houser
Enclosures

Canceling Policy

Your ultimate weapon as a consumer is to take your business elsewhere. If you have not been treated fairly by your insurance company—and repeated efforts to straighten the matter out have failed—you can cancel your policy, telling the company why you are taking this action.

You can also tell them that you will be relaying your story to the state insurance board, your friends and relations, and anyone else who wishes to listen. Since many insurance sales are made by word of mouth, the company would be wise to take your letter seriously.

September 9, 19--
Policy No. 432-56-8997

Mr. Ralph B. Selznick
President
Prentice Insurance Company
18 South LaSalle
Chicago, IL 60603

Dear Mr. Selznick:

I am writing to inform you that I have decided to cancel my policy and place my coverage with another firm. This decision comes in the wake of two years of frustrating experience with your claims department.

Over the period of two years, every time I filed a claim, the adjustor would call with a new requirement. I would meet that requirement, only to be told that I had filed late or that my claim was lost in processing. None of these charges was true, and I have the documented evidence to prove it.

Rather than go through another exhausting battle the next time I have claims to make, I have decided to change to another insurance company. Please cancel my policy and refund any premiums that may be due me.

You can be sure that all my friends, relatives, and neighbors will hear this story, as well as the state insurance board, and the consumer columnist of the Herald, who takes particular delight in alerting readers to unresponsive insurance firms. I am only sorry it took me two years to make the decision to take my business elsewhere.

Sincerely,
Joshua B. White
Joshua B. White

MEDICAL SERVICES

In today's medical environment, getting adequate medical care and finding a way to pay for it can be as complicated as many of the treatments themselves. Medicare, Medicaid, and other third-party payers flood patients and doctors alike with a mountain of forms and claims. All this can be intimidating, and you may not realize that you can have any impact on this system.

Yet as with any other service, the consumer of medical care has rights. If you are not receiving what you consider adequate treatment, you have the right to ask for an adjustment in treatment or fees. Also, you can educate yourself about the ins and outs of medical insurance forms and payment systems. If the doctor or the doctor's staff do not fill out your forms correctly, send the papers back and ask that the correct information be provided.

Finally, if a physician is seriously remiss in caring for you or someone you love, you can report the matter to your state's medical licensing board and have them investigate the situation.

Request for Insurance Information

If insurance claim reports are not filled out properly, they will not be paid. Make sure that you indicate what information the doctor must supply; include a self-addressed, stamped envelope to speed up return of the form.

January 13, 19--

Dr. Chandrika Singh
Overton Medical Clinic
147 Kedzie
Chicago, IL 60626

Dear Dr. Singh:

Would you please complete the ''Physician's Statement'' section on the enclosed insurance form? I have included a self-addressed stamped envelope for your convenience in returning the form to me.

Please notice that the form requires physicians to itemize the dates, specific treatment given, and cost per visit. I realize that this is a bit of a bother, but our group insurance plan will not pay the claim if this portion is left uncompleted.

Thank you,

Ruth Wyche

Ruth Wyche

Changing Physicians

In some cases you may need to change doctors. In your letter, briefly state the reason for the change and request that your medical records be forwarded to the new physician.

April 24, 19--

Dr. Joselyn Swooser
665 Willow Lane
Winterville, ME 00324

Dear Dr. Swooser:

Because of a recent move to Bangor, I find it necessary to change to a physician nearer our new home. I do so with great regret, as we have been very pleased with your professional services to our family over the past four years. Unfortunately, the drive to Winterville is too much for us to make on a regular basis.

Therefore, would you be kind enough to forward our medical records to Dr. Willing at the Bangor Community Hospital? The address is 7832 Redbud Lane, Bangor 00352.

Thank you for your good care, and we wish you all the best in your practice.

Regards,

Nora Winslow

Nora Winslow

Compliment for Good Service

Although we often take good medical care for granted, physicians, like everyone else, like to hear from patients when things go well. A brief note expressing your appreciation is all that's required.

July 10, 19--

Vincent A. Chiatello, M.D.
Department of Orthopedics
Clearwater Memorial Hospital
Clearwater, IA 50428

Dear Dr. Chiatello:

Just a quick note to say that everything you predicted after my surgery of three months ago has come to pass. I would like you to know how pleased I am about the outcome.

I never thought my back would feel this good again. Your post-operative advice about rest and light exercise has worked wonders. For the first time in years I'm able to sit, walk, and stand without pain.

Thank you for your superior work and care.

Sincerely,

Louella Mapes

Louella Mapes

Arranging Payment Plan

For most people, the cost of even routine tests and checkups is high, and extended medical care can be prohibitive. Few can pay the full amount when the service is given, and often insurance covers only part of the cost.

Many patients are not aware that they can arrange to pay the bill off over time. Signs that say ''Payment is expected at the time of treatment'' are usually for new patients or for those with a history of late or nonpayments. Ask the doctor or office staff to help you arrange a payment schedule so that you can pay your bill without overburdening yourself financially.

September 26, 19--

Richard Stalrock, M.D.
1500 North Seaside Lane
San Bernadino, CA 92417

Dear Dr. Stalrock:

I received your bill for my surgery of last month. As you will recall, at the time we scheduled the surgery my insurance agent assured me the procedure would be covered 100 percent under our insurance plan. I now find out that this is not the case. Our insurance will cover only 75 percent of the cost. This leaves $1300 still unpaid.

Because I have been unable to work for the past month and a half, our finances are at an all-time low. I would like to arrange to pay the remaining $1300 in monthly installments of $100, beginning in October. I hope this is satisfactory to you. If not, please let me know what other payment plan we can arrange.

Thank you,

John Hwan Chung

Complaint to State Licensing Board

If you believe a physician has been guilty of gross negligence or misconduct, you can report the matter to your state licensing board. Give enough pertinent details to inform the board about the situation and let them know you are available should they need more information.

May 13, 19--

State Board of Medical Regulation and Registration
State Capitol Building, Room 334
Springfield, IL 60001
Attention: Marsha Goodfield, M.D., Licensing Examiner

Dear Dr. Goodfield:

I wish to register a complaint about Dr. H. L. Swathmore of 645
Church Street in Highland Park, Illinois.

I consulted Dr. Swathmore on March 25 because of severe ab-
dominal pain. He questioned me about my diet and prescribed a
painkiller. The pain did not go away completely, and I consulted
him again on March 27 and again on March 29. He kept insisting
that I should stay on a light bland diet and keep taking the painkiller.

On March 31, I had to call the paramedics because of unbear-
able pain and was taken to the community hospital where I underwent an emergency appendectomy. I suffered a bout of peri-
tonitis and was very ill for four or five days.

I feel that Dr. Swathmore was totally inept in this case and should
be investigated. Acute appendicitis cannot be that hard to
diagnose—particularly since I had some of the classic symptoms.
I am considering a damage suit against him and would like to
know what action you will take in the meantime. I shudder to
think what other patient's life he may be endangering even now.

If you require further information, I can be reached at (708) 222-
2452.

Sincerely,

Mr. O. L. Abernathy
Mr. O. L. Abernathy
4169 Percy Street
Highland Park, IL 60035

VACATIONS

Good planning, and knowing where to turn for help when things go wrong, can ensure that you have a great vacation. Begin by writing the Chamber of Commerce or Visitors' Bureau of the state or location you wish to visit. They can send you information on activities, accommodations, and sites worth viewing. The tourist information office in any state capital can provide you with state road maps.

Requesting Information

The most common letters asking for information are to tourist offices and to resorts, motels, and campgrounds inquiring about accommodations and rates. In your letters, mention when you would like to visit, how many are in your family, the ages of any children, and what special interests you might have.

Although it may be quicker to call a resort for information, you may not always get as detailed an answer as in a reply to your letter query. A letter is not only cheaper than a long-distance call, but you will have rates, vacancy times, and other details in writing when you get an answer.

Requests for information about national parks can be made either from the U.S. Department of the Interior, National Park Service, Washington, DC 20240, or from individual national parks.

April 9, 19--

Chamber of Commerce
1398 West Broad Street
Louisville, KY 40202

Dear Staff:

My wife and I and our two children, ages 11 and 12, are planning a vacation to Louisville this coming July. We would like to visit some of the thoroughbred horse farms in the area.

Please send us any information you have on tours, special programs, and other events that may be scheduled during July.

Also, we would like a map of the area and a list of moderately priced motels or resorts in or around Louisville.

Thank you for your help.

Sincerely,

Eduardo A. Nuqui

Eduardo A. Nuqui
4519 North Arlington
Arlington Heights, IL 60008

Sending Reservation and Deposit

The earlier you make reservations, the better your chances of getting what you want. In sending your deposit and reservation letter, restate the accommodations you want, the dates of your stay, and the rates quoted to you. If you need to make any special arrangements for arrival or departure, be sure to mention them. Keep a copy of your letter for future reference, in case there is any question about what you wanted. Make sure you get written confirmation and a receipt for your deposit.

June 3, 19--

Broadmoor Resort
P.O. Box 2360
Brighton, NH 03223

Dear Mrs. Douglas:

Thank you for the information on your resort that you sent us. We would like to reserve a room for one week beginning Friday, October 5, and ending Saturday, October 13.

There will be four people in our party—my husband and myself and our two children, ages 3 and 7. We would like one room with two double beds. I understand your daily rate for such a room is $75.00. As required, I'm enclosing a check for $50.00 as a deposit. Please send me a confirmation of our reservation and a receipt for the deposit.

We'll arrive in the evening on Friday, October 5. Please hold our room past your usual 6 pm check-in deadline. We probably will not get there before 7 or 8 pm. We look forward to meeting you—your resort looks like a lovely place to spend a vacation. The children are very excited about visiting the animal farm nearby.

Sincerely,

Emily Carter

Emily Carter
4723 West Niles Road
New Haven, CT 06510

Requesting Items Left Behind

Even the most careful travelers can overlook important items when packing up to leave for home. If you have left something behind, or have been notified by your hotel or resort manager that you forgot to take a few things with you, be sure to enclose a check to cover the cost of mailing the items back. Give the manager the address to which you want the items shipped.

October 14, 19--

Broadmoor Resort
P.O. Box 2360
Brighton, NH 03223

Dear Mrs. Douglas:

Our warmest thanks for calling to tell us we'd left our travel packet and house keys behind. Thank goodness my husband carries duplicates of our most important keys, but you can still imagine our dismay on arriving home and finding that an entire set of keys was missing. How kind of you to contact us and relieve our anxiety.

As I promised on the phone, I'm enclosing a check to reimburse you for the cost of mailing the travel packet and keys back to us. Please address the package to:

Mr. Sergio Carter
Twin Towers, Suite 1423
4 Main Plaza
New Haven, CT 06512

Thanks again for your kindness.

Cordially,

Emily Carter

Emily Carter

Requesting Refund

When your accommodations are not what you reserved, you have a right to ask for a refund. Remember, however, that the desk clerk usually does not have the power to authorize a refund or reduction in rates when the hotel, motel, or resort makes a mistake. Only the manager or vice president can do so. Write your letter to these individuals, explaining what happened and what you want them to do.

June 15, 19--

Mr. Hendrick Campbell, Manager
SeaSide Hotel
346 Flamingo Road
Tampa Bay, FL 33602

Dear Mr. Campbell:

On the evening of June 1, my husband and I arrived at your hotel with reservations for a double room. The desk clerk informed us that no room was available because of a convention in town. Even though we had reserved our room one month in advance, we were now told that no rooms were vacant in the entire hotel. In fact, there were no rooms available anywhere in town. We spent the night in your hotel lobby, sleeping on (and off) one of the couches.

The second evening, the convention guests left and we were given our double room. As if the disappointment in our accommodations were not enough, imagine our disgust when we received our monthly credit card statement and discovered we had been charged full price for both nights: $125.00 per night.

We did not stay in our room both nights, Mr. Campbell. In fact, since your hotel accepted our reservation and then failed to provide the promised room, we believe we should not be charged at all for having to sleep in your hotel lobby.

Please credit $125.00 to our credit card account (MC 1234-5678-9000-0000). We would appreciate your prompt attention in this matter.

Sincerely,

Mrs. Anthony Caparelli

Mrs. Anthony Caparelli

Canceling Vacation Plans

When you must cancel vacation plans, put the cancellation in writing, even if you telephone first to say you can't make the dates you reserved. Restate the plans you originally made and the amount of deposit or other monies that should be refunded to you. Apologize for any inconvenience the cancellation may cause your hosts.

August 13, 19--

Mr. Thomas Castlebury
Castlebury Day Tours
Napa, CA 94558

Dear Mr. Castlebury:

As I explained on the telephone this morning, I will be unable to go on your September 12 tour of Napa Valley wineries. Unfortunately, I have been called for jury duty on that date. I have enclosed a photocopy of my jury notification.

I am very disappointed that I will miss the tour. I hope I will be able to participate the next fall. Please return my $82.00 payment for the tour, which I made in advance.

I apologize for any inconvenience this may have caused you.

Yours truly,

Rita Mae Ling

Rita Mae Ling

CHAPTER
≡SEVEN

CIVIC CONCERNS

As a citizen or member of your community, state, and nation, you have certain powers and rights. Your opinions, suggestions, and concerns regarding your place of worship, political matters, neighbors, the media, schools, and other activities can make a difference. The model letters in the following sections show you how to put your interests and concerns into words.

PLACE OF WORSHIP

A place of worship serves as the focus of many people's spiritual and social lives. Ministers, rabbis, priests, and other religious workers occupy a unique position as counselors, advisors, friends, and leaders.

Your letters can do much to foster open communication between you and the leaders of your religious community. Whether you are expressing a need, a concern, or a compliment, a well-written letter can help you.

The correct forms of address for various religious leaders and workers are given in Chapter 4, under the section "Religious Orders."

Welcoming New Clergy

When a new minister, rabbi, or priest arrives, a letter of welcome can help put the new person at ease and give you an opportunity to introduce yourself and your family.

June 28, 19--

Dear Reverend Thompson,

My family and I want to welcome you to our congregation here in Wheatley. All of us look forward to your leadership of our church, and we are anxious to get to know you and your family. The folks in Lebron said many good things about your work in their church, particularly with the young people.

We hope that the friends you make here will be as treasured as those you left behind in Lebron. We're glad you've chosen to come to us. Please know that we are ready to help in any way in the weeks ahead.

Yours sincerely,

Frank and Merretta Gutierrez

Request for Clergy Participation

Clergy are often asked to speak before different groups on a variety of spiritual, ethical, or moral topics, or to offer an invocation and blessing at a dinner or banquet. If you are responsible for inviting a religious leader to attend your function, be sure you state clearly what you would like him or her to do. Mention if you are offering an honorarium or if you would like the person to volunteer his or her services. Finally, try to give the person at least two weeks' notice before the date of the event.

May 13, 19--

Dear Rabbi Solenstein:

On behalf of Boy Scout Troop 545, I would like to request your participation in our annual community recognition banquet. We would like to have you give an invocation before the meal and a blessing or benediction at the end of the evening.

The banquet will be held at Holden Towers Restaurant, 1200 Central Street, on Wednesday evening, June 3rd, at 6:30 pm. We usually finish all ceremonies within two hours, so you should be free by no later than 9:00 pm.

Unfortunately, our finances do not permit us to offer honorariums to speakers we invite, but we hope you will be able to accept our invitation. Three of our scouts are members of your temple congregation and have spoken highly of you.

Please call me at 224–5533, evenings, to let me know if you will be able to join us. We would appreciate your presence.

Sincerely,

Greg Delvecchio
Troop 545 Leader

Letter from Search or Call Committee

In most Protestant denominations, the process of finding a new minister is generally entrusted to a special board or search committee within the church. When a prospective candidate has been found, the chairperson of the committee often makes the first contact by letter. The letter should state the position available, give a brief description of the church, and outline what is expected of the person who heads the church.

June 9, 19--

Dear Dr. Carol Lombard:

Covenant Church of Little Rock, Arkansas, is searching for a replacement for our senior minister, Dr. Frederick Roberts, who will retire this fall. We have heard from a number of people about your exceptional abilities, and we would like you to address our congregation as a candidate. If our offer interests you, we invite you and Mr. Lombard to visit us at a mutually convenient time.

I have enclosed a brochure that describes the history of our church, a membership directory, four recent church bulletins, and a booklet we give to visitors and prospective members. Our staff consists of a Youth Minister, a Director of Religious Education, Director of Music, and two clerical workers.

Our resident membership is about 300, with about 220 active members. Because our church is located in a university town, we have considerable turnover in our membership. However, there is still the potential for significant growth in our church. We would like to have a minister, like yourself, who strongly believes in outreach and evangelism.

Please give our invitation your prayerful consideration. You can call me collect at 332-5689 during business hours or 332-4519 evenings, or write to the address above. If you decide to accept our invitation, we will forward plane tickets for you and Mr. Lombard to visit our town.

Very truly yours,

Carolyn Younger

Carolyn Younger
Chairperson, Search Committee

Letter of Call to Clergy Candidate

A letter of call amounts to a job offer to a candidate. The church congregation votes on which candidate they want to offer the position, and a letter is sent detailing the salary, housing, vacation time, and benefits. Often a separate job description accompanies the letter.

August 2, 19--

Dear Dr. Carol Lombard:

Thank you for coming to Covenant Church two weeks ago. We were delighted to have you and Mr. Lombard spend time with us.

As chairperson of the Search Committee, I have the honor and privilege of extending to you a formal invitation to become the Senior Minister at Covenant Church.

You will be pleased to know that the congregation voted nearly unanimously in favor of calling you to our church. The congregation has also agreed on the terms of the contract we discussed while you were here. Details of housing, salary, vacation time, insurance benefits, and other items are covered in the enclosed sheet.

We look forward to your coming to Covenant Church. If you have any questions, please call me. When we receive your letter of acceptance, we will arrange for the parsonage to be ready for you and your family by November 1. As we discussed, you would then begin your ministry with us on November 15.

Yours sincerely,

Carolyn Younger

Carolyn Younger
Chairperson, Search Committee

Letter of Termination

It may become necessary for a congregation to write a letter of termination, asking the religious leader to resign. Such letters require tact and discretion while firmly stating the congregation's position.

April 19, 19--

Dear Dr. Abernathy:

As chairperson of the Board of Deacons, I have to advise you that the congregation at its meeting yesterday voted to request that you submit your resignation from Wellington Church.

This is a difficult, painful decision, but you have been aware of the complaints of the congregation over the past six months. The promised changes have not materialized. The specific objections are the level of outside political activity you maintain to the detriment of your ministry here at the church. We respect your beliefs and views, but object to your repeated absences and to your use of the church as a political forum.

The congregation has voted to continue your compensation and other benefits for a period of two months from today. At that time, we ask that you vacate the parsonage. You will be paid for vacation time that has not been used and be provided with severance pay equivalent to one week's pay for each month you have served the church. The Director of Christian Education will assume responsibility for services beginning next Sunday.

We deeply regret the necessity for this action and will always remember fondly the many good things you accomplished during your time with us. We wish you the best in locating a suitable position commensurate with your abilities and political interests.

Sincerely,

Julius Austin

Julius Austin, Chairman

Requesting Clergy Replacement

Although many mainstream denominations have their clergy selected for them, if the match is incompatible, the congregation can request that the person be replaced. The letter should include specific reasons and facts about why the individual should be replaced and must be signed by all those willing to validate what has been said.

October 3, 19--

Dear Bishop Tyler:

It is with great regret that we, the active members of St. Angelica's, have decided to ask that Father Joseph DeMara be relieved of his duties in this parish.

His five years with us have been marked by his repeated outbursts against members of the congregation and his erratic behavior regarding church programs. On numerous occasions we had scheduled church activities only to have Father DeMara cancel them. At other times, he has accused members of the congregation of conspiring to have him removed from his position, and even made one tirade the subject of a sermon. The children are afraid to approach him anymore.

The parishoners who have signed this letter do so out of a deep concern for the spiritual welfare of this church. Each person is prepared to talk to church authorities about these issues.

We are sorry to have to take this action, and pray that you will replace Father DeMara with a strong spiritual leader. This congregation is in need of healing.

Respectfully yours,

(Signers)

GOVERNMENT OFFICIALS

In the United States, government officials at the local, state, or federal level are accountable to the voters who elect them. Although telephones and fax machines make communicating with elected officials easier, it is still the well-written letter that can make the greatest impact. Politicians admit privately that a personal letter from a constituent carries more weight than any other form of communication.

Regardless of whom you are writing, keep the following guidelines in mind. These brief do's and don'ts can help you write an effective letter that gets your point across to your elected representative.

DO:

► Keep your letter brief—no more than a page or two.

► Address only one issue—this guarantees that your letter goes to the right staff member.

► Make your letter personal—if you have met the official, contributed to the election campaign, and voted for him or her, mention this in your letter.

► Get right to the point—let the official know what your concern is and what you would like the person to do about it.

► Demonstrate your knowledge of the official's past record— refer to the voting record, stand on issues, or other items; note what you consider praiseworthy as it relates to your concern.

► Ask for the official's position or a copy of any bills you are concerned about.

► Follow up any answer—if the elected representative writes back, let him or her know if you are satisfied with the response.

► Include your name and address, along with your congressional district or ward.

► Keep copies of every letter you send and receive.

DON'T:

► Don't apologize for writing or taking up the person's time— your legislators are there to represent you.

► Never try to impress the official with your importance or exaggerate your case—legislators can see through these manipulative techniques.

► Don't threaten to oppose a legislator at an election—such threats are resented, not feared, and usually have no effect.

► Don't hestitate to take a strong stand. However, don't unleash your anger—although the letter will be a release for you, it won't be appreciated by the official. *How* you say something can drown out *what* you say.

► Never send a carbon copy or pre-printed postcard—it implies that the official is not as important as the person who received the original or the person who merits a personal letter.

The correct forms of address for government officials are given in Chapter 4.

Letter to U.S. President

Expressing a concern to the President is every citizen's right. Although letters to the president are generally read by aides, your opinion matters. Part of the aides' responsibilities involve letting the president know how people in the country feel about what is being done or proposed. Your letter will be added to the overall picture of public opinion.

June 11, 19--

Dear Mr. President:

    I am greatly disturbed by your reported plan to promote the development of offshore oil drilling sites on the California coast, the Gulf of Mexico, and the New Jersey shore.

    I strongly urge you to consider the environmental hazards in drilling near these heavily settled areas. The devastating effects of the Prince William Sound spill would be multiplied many times over should such an accident occur in these waters. We have already seen that neither the oil companies nor government agencies have been able to contain damage in these cases.

    It is time to institute conservation measures that provide long-term solutions to our energy needs without jeopardizing our environment. I urge you to assert your leadership in such an effort and to stop the expansion of offshore drilling efforts.

Very truly yours,

R. T. Flanders

R. T. Flanders

Letter to House Committee Member

Legislation in the House of Representatives generally originates in one of the committees or subcommittees of the House. When writing to express your opinion about a bill, your letter should be sent to the chair of that committee or to your own congressperson who is a member of the committee.

In your letter, refer to the bill's number if you know it. You can find out the legislation number by calling your congressperson's local office. If you are protesting a particular provision in a bill, urge your representative to delete this section or to replace it with a better provision.

August 3, 19--

The Honorable Daniel Ritter
Chairman, House Ways and Means Committee
House of Representatives
Washington, DC 20510

Dear Mr. Ritter:

I am all for tax reform, but one part of the new legislation being considered is grossly unfair to freelance writers and photographers. The Tax Reform Act (H.R. 3467) contains a provision requiring authors to utilize uniform capitalization in their annual tax returns.

This provision, meant to apply to manufacturing businesses, places an impossible burden on authors. It requires that we defer taking deductions for work-related expenses until the year in which we earn money from our books. Since book development can take up to three or four (or more) years, we would be unable to deduct any expenses for creating these works during that time. Many independent writers and scholars would be financially unable to complete their work.

I understand that a Technical Tax Corrections Measure (H.R. 3445) recommends that authors be exempted from this provision in the Tax Reform Act. I strongly urge you to support passage of the corrections measure. Thank you.

Yours sincerely,

Lorraine Huer

Lorraine Huer

Letter to Senator

You may wish to write your senator about pending legislation. On occasion, you may feel that your senator has voted on the wrong side of a bill. If the bill has not yet been approved or is up for another vote, you can write a letter urging the senator to change his or her vote. Be sure you state your reasons clearly and do not simply engage in an emotional tirade against the senator's voting record. If appropriate, recognize the individual's support for similar bills in the past. Remember to refer to the bill by number whenever possible.

May 3, 19--

The Honorable Margaret Hansen
United States Senate
Washington, DC 20510

Dear Senator Hansen:

I urge you to consider and vote against the Long-term Health Care Bill (S. 234). I am currently a resident in Morningside Nursing Home in Baton Rouge, Louisiana. As a constituent who is directly affected by this legislation, I am opposed to the law as it now reads.

It does not address the primary concern of most nursing home residents—the cost of medications and extra medical care beyond that already provided by the nursing homes. We must pay for such services out of a fixed income that is declining in value every year. We need some relief against the rising cost of medications and additional care.

I urge you to vote against S. 234 and support Senator Homes's bill, S. 592, which places a limit on fees charged to nursing home residents for medication and extra medical care. Your fine record of supporting measures to ease the financial burden on senior citizens indicates your concern about this issue. Please help us once again. Thank you.

Sincerely yours,

Cordwaine Miller

Cordwaine Miller

Letter to Governor

As the highest executive in the state, the governor has the power to influence the actions of state and local officials. Be sure that the issue you take to the governor cannot be settled at a lower level. Your concern should be one that requires the use of the governor's power or that can be handled most effectively by this official's staff.

March 4, 19--

The Honorable Clarissa G. Byrnes
Capitol Building
Sacramento, CA 95814

Dear Governor Byrnes:

I am deeply concerned about the current state labor laws concerning migrant workers and their families. As these laws now stand, migrant workers are not guaranteed even the basic rights of housing and education.

Specifically, I am appalled by the stories of migrant workers reported in the Sacramento Times. The children of these families work ten to twelve hours a day and have little schooling beyond the third grade. Housing and medical care are clearly substandard, and working conditions are dangerous in the extreme.

I urge you to take action to have new labor laws drafted that would guarantee migrant workers the fundamental necessities of decent housing and education. The citizens of this state should not tolerate conditions that resemble economic slavery. I will watch with interest your actions on this matter—as I'm sure many others will.

Sincerely,

Geno Bassinger
Geno Bassinger

Letter to Mayor

The mayor of your city is often the best person to contact for a situation that lies outside your own alderperson's jurisdiction. The mayor directs the activities of the city's departments and services, often appointing the directors or supervisors of these agencies. By taking your complaint straight to the top, you may be able to get action faster than if you go through the lower levels of city bureaucracy.

October 12, 19--

The Honorable Marian Isner
City Hall
Cleveland, OH 44114

Dear Mayor Isner:

I must ask you to correct a dangerous condition at Lake and Colonial streets that has already caused three traffic accidents in the past two weeks.

The traffic control light at this intersection was removed three months ago for some unknown reason, and stop signs were installed in its place. Yet thick hedges on Colonial prevent oncoming westbound traffic from being able to see cars driving through the intersection until they are almost on top of them. Since this intersection is crowded at rush hour, the potential for serious accidents is high.

Just last Tuesday a two-car collision at this corner injured two young children in one of the cars and totaled both vehicles. Would you please bring your good offices to bear on this problem and have the traffic light reinstalled? It will help the rush hour situation and could very well save a number of lives.

Thank you,

Rita Towers-Gutierrez
Rita Towers-Gutierrez

Letter to Alderman/woman

Your alderman or alderwoman is the elected official closest to your neighborhood and precinct. He or she can be called on to handle any number of problems, from garbage collection to tenant-landlord disputes to summer activities for neighborhood youth. It is well worth your time to get to know this individual. He or she may be quicker to respond when you express a concern.

August 19, 19--

Alderwoman Anne Rainey
1235 South Evert
Lake Forest, IL 60035

Dear Ms. Rainey:

Despite several calls over the past three weeks, I am unable to get either the police or Department of Streets and Sanitation to do anything about the two abandoned cars on my block. The cars are unsightly and a hazard for youngsters—vandals have taken the tires and smashed the windshields, leaving broken glass all over the street.

Can you help us get these cars towed away? Our neighborhood should not be a dumping ground for whatever people feel like throwing away. Thank you for what I am sure will be your prompt action.

Sincerely,

Aaron Pilsen

Aaron Pilsen
103rd Ward, 4th precinct

Request for Absentee Ballot

If you are going to be away at the time of an election in your city, state, or country, you can request an absentee ballot to cast your vote. Write to your county elections board or elections commission to send you the proper form. In this way you can have a voice in any election. Be sure you meet the deadlines for sending in your ballot, or your vote will be invalid.

January 14, 19--

Chair of the Cook County Elections Commission
County Building
Yorkville, Arkansas 45678

Dear Chairperson:

I will be in England during the next gubernatorial election on March 3rd. Please send me an absentee ballot, plus instructions on how to fill out the form and where to mail it.

Send the form to my home address, 338 Dilberry Lane, Yorkville, 45769. If there is any further information I need in order to have my vote count in this election, please let me know. Thank you.

Sincerely,

Evelyn Underwood Hill

Evelyn Underwood Hill

Internal Revenue Service

Contrary to popular opinion, the IRS is not an anti-taxpayer agency. You can approach the IRS to arrange installment payments to pay your tax bill, get an error in billing corrected, or get help for your tax questions. In contacting the IRS, be sure to include your taxpayer identification number (Social Security number), the tax year you are referring to, and your document locator number, if you have a record of it. Keep a copy of all correspondence with the IRS.

July 15, 19--

Taxpayer Identification number: 084–34–0536
Form: 1040
Tax Year Ending: 12–31–89
Document Locator No. 09221–120–5664–3

Internal Revenue Service
P.O. Box 8620
Prairie Village, KS 66208

Attention: Chief, Taxpayer Assistance Section

My 1989 tax bill was unexpectedly large, and I could not pay the full amount on April 15. I would like to pay the remaining amount, $1,356, in monthly installments beginning August 1, as follows:

Payment 1, August 1	$374.00
Payment 2, September 1	$374.00
Payment 3, October 1	$374.00
Payment 4, November 1	$374.00
Total	$1356.00

I have already paid in $2,500 toward the total amount due, $3,656. Please let me know if this payment schedule is satisfactory.

Sincerely,

H. R. Kincaid

H. R. Kincaid

Deferment or Dismissal from Jury Duty

Although it is part of every citizen's duty to respond to a jury summons, there are times when jury service is a hardship. You can petition to postpone your jury duty or to be excused from having to serve. Your jury summons often contains instructions on how to go about requesting a postponement or dismissal. The following model letters illustrate the procedure.

July 11, 19--

Skokie Court
5600 Old Orchard Road
Room 111
Skokie, IL 60077

Dear Jury Service Office:

I am writing in response to the enclosed Summons to Appear for Jury Service, which I received recently. The jury number assigned to me was 7185338-2-69, and the service date shown was 7-22 at 9:30 am.

I am petitioning the court to defer my jury service until January 19--. I am presently unemployed and am in the midst of looking for a job.

I called the Jury Service Department at the Court last week to let them know of my circumstances. I was told to write this letter of explanation to the Court.

Thank you for your consideration and acceptance of this special request for deferment.

Sincerely,

Augustine Morgan
Augustine Morgan

MEDIA MESSAGES

Radio, TV, and the print media (newspapers, magazines, journals) are highly sensitive to public likes and dislikes. In television and radio, a sophisticated system of rating points measures audience size and preferences. Media executives use these figures to determine how much to charge advertisers to air their commercials at various times during the night and day. Competition for prime-time spots is fierce. With so much at stake, it's no surprise that media executives and their commercial sponsors pay close attention to public responses to their programming.

If you are offended by a show, want to offer a suggestion, or appreciate a program, don't hesitate to write the station. Call the station switchboard to find out who is the program director or general manager and address your letter to that individual. Include the call letters of the station or network in the inside address.

The following model letters cover several situations in which you may want to contact a radio or television station.

Radio

The program director is responsible for the format of a radio show—whether it is all rock music; a mix of music styles, talk shows, and consumer advice; or a classical station. If you have a compliment or complaint, the program director is the one who can take action on your letter.

Many stations have adopted their format because of ratings and economic factors and not for aesthetic reasons or personal preference. Your protest or suggestion may not make a difference. On the other hand, you do have a final recourse: Turn the dial to another station.

Music Request. Requests for particular music or specific songs can be made either to the station manager (or program director) or to the disk jockey or radio announcer who hosts the show during the time you want your request played. If possible, state both the title and recording artist of the song you want to hear and the time you would like it to be played.

May 10, 19--

Maria Donahue
c/o WBEZ-AM
723 West Walkup Road
Arlington, VA 22206

Dear Ms. Donahue:

I really enjoy your show and listen to it faithfully every evening. I would like to request a special song for my brother—"Miracles" by Gayle Preston—during the last hour of your show on Tuesday, May 12.

At that time my brother will be over at our house for dinner. He has just finished a cross-country bicycle tour, and "Miracles" describes very well how we feel about his making the trip safely home. If you can, mention his name, James Perkins, and say that the song is dedicated to him by his family. I hope you can do this—it would mean a lot to us all.

Sincerely,

Marjorie Perkins
Marjorie Perkins

Programming Suggestion. You may have a special interest or need that you would like to see your radio station address. Put your suggestion in writing and send it to the program director. If the station likes your idea, you may tune in to hear a show that you helped start.

June 29, 19--

Amos Halyard
Station Manager
KYRD-FM
490 Curtain Lane
Salt Lake City, UT 84120

Dear Mr. Halyard:

There is a need out here that your station could fill. Ask your-self what is more widely found in homes and offices than even computers or VCRs? Answer: the potted plant. But are these plants healthy and growing? Many times not. I think a weekly or semi-weekly mid-morning or evening program on basic indoor plant care would be a big hit with your listeners.

Rather than overwhelm your audience with agricultural infor-mation, take a light approach to the subject. Call the programs "Greens for Greenhorns" or "Growing Pains" or "A New Leaf." Put some fun into describing plants and plant care—for example, educating people on how to tell a succulent from a bromeliad or how not to kill their croton with kindness.

The program could touch on little-known topics like the effect of office music or electromagnetic fields on plants. You could even have a call-in segment for people to ask questions and share their experiences and home remedies. Doesn't this sound like a winner? I think so.

Yours truly,

Randell G. Lee

Randell G. Lee

Television

Television has considerable power to influence our attitudes and con-ception of the world around us. As a viewer, you can have a voice in how that influence is used. Some stations are even required by federal law to provide ordinary citizens with rebuttal time on the air to management editorials.

With the advent of cable, the number of stations has mushroomed, and with it the range of programs offered. You can exercise your rights as a citizen by expressing your views about what you see on television to TV management and sponsors.

Protesting a TV Program. If you find a particular show or weekly program objectionable, say so either to the program manager or directly to the sponsors of the show. You can obtain the names and addresses of sponsors from the public library. Although station managers may or may not respond to your letter, sponsors generally are sensitive to viewers who link their products with an offensive program. A sponsor's threat to withdraw its commercials from a show may force some changes in the program's format and content.

November 7, 19--

Mr. Sander Shapiro
Station Manager
KEB Television Network
891 Broadway
Los Angeles, CA 90024

Dear Mr. Shapiro:

Your station has just lost me and my family as viewers on Thursday evening. We are so offended by your new situation comedy show "Hold the Plow" that we will avoid your station for the entire evening.

Since the program is about rural life, and we come from that background, we eagerly tuned in the show. What a bust. The program portrays farmers and rural life in a silly, trivial way without ever letting viewers know how truly difficult and dangerous this life is. Members of your audience who know rural life will undoubtedly share my opinion, while others will be greatly misinformed by what they see.

In addition, the people starring in the sitcom are completely unbelievable as rural folks. Not only are they too "perfect" looking (apparently no one ever steps in anything, and no one ever sweats), but they talk like transplanted New Yorkers. Even "Beverly Hillbillies" had more realism than this show.

Please plow under "Hold the Plow." Thank you.

Sincerely,

Wendy & Stephen Pulliam
Wendy and Stephen Pulliam

Commending a TV Program. It's as important to write in support of what you like as it is to protest what you find offensive. Good programming needs to be affirmed so that management will continue to provide it. Again, a letter to both the station manager and the sponsor is appropriate.

April 12, 19--

Mr. Arthur M. Najarian
Vice President, Public Relations
Apple Paper Co.
866 N. Maple Road
Boston, MA 02152

Dear Mr. Najarian:

I would like to thank you for sponsoring the television documentary series "The American City," broadcast through March on WKET Channel 9.

Over the past several years, various networks have tried to deal with the changes taking place in our cities, but "The American City" struck me as the best of the lot. It showed the complex economic structure that fosters some of the worse abuses of city government power, as well as the forces working to improve urban life.

You may get some complaints from people whose toes got stepped on, but I believe the presentation did a good job balancing conflicting viewpoints. Well done! I hope you continue to sponsor such outstanding work.

Sincerely yours,

April Albietz

April Albietz

cc: Program Director
WKET Channel 9

Requesting Rebuttal Time.   When a television station presents an editorial by the station's management, the station is required by Federal Communications Commission regulations to provide free rebuttal time to a responsible member of the opposing point of view. If you would like to offer your rebuttal to a recent editorial, write the station manager requesting time. Be willing to discuss the text of your remarks with the manager.

July 23, 19––

Ms. Louise Weston
General Manager
WYET Television Station
560 North Michigan
Chicago, IL 60601

Dear Ms. Weston:

I was impressed last night with your station's editorial arguing against the proposed city ordinance to ban smoking in all public areas. However, I happen to be strongly on the other side of this issue and have documentation for my position. I would like to take advantage of your invitation to viewers to make a rebuttal.

As a physician, I have forty years' experience both in clinical research and general practice to support why the city ordinance should be passed. If you are willing to consider my proposal, please inform me about the procedures, the amount of time available, and possible dates for taping my remarks. If you can furnish a transcript of your editorial, it would be helpful in preparing my remarks.

I am willing to submit my text for advance review or to discuss my proposed argument with you or your representatives by telephone.

Sincerely yours,

Patricia Beckjord, M.D.

Patricia Beckjord, M.D.

Newspapers/Magazines

Letters to the editor provide a forum for readers to express their opinions, suggestions, and complaints. Most publications will not publish anonymous letters. Use the inverted pyramid sequence in your letter, coming right to the point, and then supporting your position with details. Double-check your facts, names, and dates, and be sure you correctly cite any articles or editorials that appeared earlier in the publication. Sign your correct name and address. An editor may wish to verify that you are truly the author of the letter before printing it.

Local and national newspapers devote a special section, usually on the editorial-opinion (known as the op-ed) page, to letters from readers. Address your letter to the managing editor of the paper. Keep your letter brief and focused. Editors usually reserve the right to omit parts of your letter if they do not have space to print all of it and to change your wording to clarify or condense your thoughts. However, the essence of what you say will be preserved.

Many magazines also offer a "letter to the editor" section for their readers. The same guidelines apply to these letters as to newspaper letters. Be sure of your facts when you write. The editors usually reserve the right to edit your letter for length and style.

February 16, 19--

Mrs. Cathy Thomchik
Managing Editor
<u>Morning Post</u>
358 Church Street
Macon, GA 31256

Dear Mrs. Thomchik:

I am all in support of the new library but strongly object to the proposed location at Ridge and Main. This site is five blocks from the nearest public transportation—a long way for children and older people to walk.

Parking would also be a problem at the proposed site. The planners admit that street parking will have to supplement the meager lot that goes with the site. Unfortunately, Lee High School nearby has night classes, and cars already fill up the street spaces as far north as the proposed site.

The library committee should hold public hearings to consider other locations for the library. The vacant lot at Howard and Beech, for example, is a much more convenient site. If we can't find a better spot than Ridge and Main, then perhaps we should look at who stands to benefit from the new library—the public or the Ridge/Main property owner?

Sincerely,

Dorothy Malone, Esq.

Dorothy Malone, Esq.
Younger, Strachen & Lee Attorneys at Law
67 East Oriole Blvd.
Macon, GA 31255

NEIGHBORS

Home and property represent a substantial investment in anyone's life, making relations with neighbors an important part of home ownership. It's important to know how to handle problems, disputes, or difficulties with neighbors. In most cases you will be able to deal with these issues personally or over the telephone.

There are times, however, when a letter may be the best way to communicate your concerns or compliments. A letter allows you to state your case without interruption and to propose solutions or make suggestions that the recipient has time to think over. You can follow up your letter with a visit or phone call.

Avoid venting your anger by being patronizing, sarcastic, or flippant. Assume that there is some way to work things out amicably. Don't threaten court action or any legal recourse unless you have no choice.

Complaints

You need to exercise sensitivity when approaching people about their pets' behavior. Many people feel more strongly attached to their animals than to other people. Yet owners are responsible for training their pets and ensuring that they do not bother other people. When they fail in this obligation, their animals can become a nuisance. In your letter, state clearly what you would like the owner to do.

A neighbor's party that keeps you awake at night is no fun. If it is a regular occurrence or happens often enough to be annoying, and if a simple complaint does nothing to change the situation, you may need to write a letter. State your case clearly, citing the number of times you were disturbed and what you would like your neighbor to do about the situation.

September 22, 19--

Dear Mr. and Mrs. Trimble,

I don't know if you realize that your children, Rob and Sandra, throw rather extravagant parties when you are out of town, but your neighbors always know.

We are awakened usually around midnight by a boombox sound that shakes the walls. This no sooner subsides than the partygoers take the party outside. People are laughing or crying or fighting in the street outside your house until we either tell them to stop or we call the police. Even when the party breaks up we get no relief. Sometimes they stage a drag race down the middle of our block.

We are not against young people having fun — so long as it is kept within reasonable bounds. Please talk to your children about toning the parties down or having them supervised by adults. This has always been a friendly neighborhood, and we'd like to keep it that way. We would not want the police to close down the parties.

Sincerely yours,
Al and Bertha Harris

Asking for a Favor

When you need help, it can be comforting to know you can turn to your neighbors. When asking for a favor, state explicitly what you need, when you need it, and for how long. If there is likely to be an expense involved, arrange to have money available beforehand.

May 20, 19--

Dear Gary and Jackie,

Craig and I will be gone four weeks this summer from June 1 to July 1 to take care of my sister's children while she and her husband are in Washington, DC. We would like to ask if you could watch our house and take care of the garden for the time we are gone.

We will take care of mail, newspapers, telephone, and delivery services. All you would need to do would be to water the plants once a week, air the house out, mow, and water the lawn once a week.

We would really appreciate it if you could do this for us. Take it for granted that we will volunteer to *watch your house in return whenever you have to be away for any length of time. Let us know if you can house-sit for the month of June.*

Thanks,

Arlene Sample

Joining in Protest

If a neighbor's activities are getting out of hand and bothering everyone on the block, united action may be the only way to confront the individual. Organize your effort so that one letter speaks for you all. State your grievance firmly, and indicate the consequences if the neighbor fails to respond. Make sure you have researched your legal recourse before writing the letter. You want to get results, not make empty threats.

October 14, 19--

Dear Mr. McDonald,

Several of us have spoken to you individually about the collection of broken motors and equipment in your front and backyard, but so far the unsightly mess is still in full view. Although we have nothing against people starting their own repair business, our block is not zoned for private businesses.

In addition, the broken equipment catches rain water and makes a perfect breeding ground for mosquitoes and other pests. It also attracts rats, raccoons, possums, stray cats and dogs, and other animal pests that are becoming a real nuisance to the rest of us. Over the past two weeks, all of us have had our garbage cans ripped open and garbage strewn over our yards.

If the motors and equipment are not removed by the end of next week, we will be forced to call in the city officials. If you need help hauling the stuff away, we'd be glad to lend a hand. We'll be talking to you this coming weekend about clearing up this whole matter so we can get our neighborhood looking good again.

Your Elm Street Neighbors,

(signatures)

Property Line Dispute

A property line dispute can touch off hard feelings between neighbors. You need to have the facts straight before approaching your neighbor with your concern. Take the attitude that you can work out the situation, but be prepared to back up your claim with legal help. A letter may be the best way to lay out the facts; it can serve as a document of your dispute should it have to be settled in court.

April 20, 19--

Dear Ms. Appleby,

We have been neighbors for five years now and always enjoyed good relations. At this point, I find I must write about a concern that is becoming more troublesome as time goes on.

Although you have clearly marked your property line along the back lawn, this line seems to disappear once it gets to the end of the lot and into the parking spaces by our two garages in the alleyway. Your guests frequently park their cars so they overlap onto our property and block out our garbage cans and sometimes even our garage door. Getting our car out of the garage is sometimes a major problem.

Although we have mentioned the problem to you, the situation hasn't changed. Only last Monday we missed a garbage pickup because one of your guest's cars hid our cans from sight and the sanitation truck drove on past.

Perhaps we could solve the problem by constructing a joint fence between our two garages. We could split the expense and eliminate the hassle for both of us. You would no longer have to remind your guests where to park, and we would no longer have our garbage cans and garage blocked off. I'll call you later this week to talk this over. It could be that in this case good fences will make good neighbors.

Sincerely,

Deborah and Eugene Woltering
Deborah and Eugene Woltering

POLICE AND FIRE DEPARTMENTS

Although in most cases you will phone the police department or fire department to request help or report an emergency, there are occasions when a letter is warranted. A written request or concern has a better chance of reaching a higher-ranking official than does a phone call. If your telephone calls have not gotten results, or if you want to give more detail, put your concern in writing.

Requesting Help with a Local Problem

When you want the police department to get involved with a local problem, write to the police chief or captain. Describe the situation and state what you would like the police to do.

May 9, 19--

Chief Alan B. Lundberg
Atlanta Police Department
43 South Main
Atlanta, GA 30309

Dear Chief Lundberg,

I live in the Lamamore Park area on Elm Street, and I would like to call your attention to a problem that has all of us in the area greatly concerned. Over the past six months, we have noticed increasing evidence of gang activity in and around Lamamore Park. Graffiti has been scrawled across alley walls, garage doors, apartment entranceways, and the transit stop. The two gangs involved appear to be the Cobras and the Kings.

Neighbors over on Sherman have reported gang fights in the park late at night. One of the houses near the park is reported to be a drug house where kids of all ages can buy any drug they want. Many of the kids are afraid to go to the park even during the day because gang members hang around the playground area.

We need your help to stop the gangs while they are just getting started. Some of us have formed a Lamamore Neighbors Association, and we want the police to help us patrol the area and organize some summer activities for the kids. The busier we keep them, the less time they'll have to fight or join in a gang. Call me at 439-2738 to set up a time that Lamamore Neighbors can meet with you and other police officials.

Sincerely,

Abner Cole

Abner Cole

Reporting Suspicious Activity

Many crimes are solved or prevented by information citizens provide. Often people will not have solid reasons for their suspicions— just a feeling that something's wrong.

Police crime prevention departments urge people to report anything that seems suspicious to them. Direct your letter to the chief of police, the desk sergeant, the crime detection or crime prevention bureau or to your neighborhood patrol officer.

September 26, 19--

Dear Sergeant Howard:

I may have seen too many Hitchcock movies in my time, but I think there is something strange going on in the 1300 block of Wilmont Avenue.

Normally this block is very quiet, but about three weeks ago I began to notice that several cars, each a few minutes apart, began pulling up to the corner of Wilmont and Orange between the hours of 11 pm and 1 am. First, a van parks a few feet from the stop sign, and then these other cars, one at a time, pull up beside it. The drivers chat a few minutes, exchange something, and then the car drives away.

I would like someone to look into this. Probably it's nothing more than kids hanging out, but I would feel easier if you investigated this for yourselves. Thank you.

Sincerely,

Bill Constantine

Bill Constantine

Thanks for Service

When you have received prompt action from the police or fire department, a brief note thanking them is a courtesy. Like other civil service employees, police and firefighters tend to hear more often when things go wrong than when things go right.

August 15, 19--

Captain R. L. Chirico
Fleming Fire Department
1390 West Hinman
Fleming, CO 70834

Dear Captain Chirico:

I would like you to know what a superior job your paramedics did last night, August 14, in responding to our emergency.

My elderly father suffered what seemed to be a heart attack about 6:30 pm. We called the paramedics, who arrived here in what seemed like two minutes. They were very efficient and kind, administering medication as directed by the emergency room at Memorial Hospital. All the while, they were talking to my father, reassuring him that he would be all right. They got him stabilized and the rest of us calmed down, then they transported my father and myself to the hospital.

My father is doing quite well today, and I am sure it is because your paramedics were so well trained. In the flurry of activity I neglected to get their names, but I would like them to know how grateful we are for the kind of service they gave us. Please convey our gratitude to them.

Sincerely,

Marianne C. Poppen

Marianne C. Poppen
1876 North Cotton Road

Requesting a Speaker

Police officers and firefighters are often requested as speakers at schools, youth groups, senior citizen homes, community gatherings, and other organizational meetings. When you are asking for a speaker, be sure to outline clearly what you want the individual to cover, how long he or she will have to talk, and the age and interest level of the audience. Make your request to the fire chief or police chief or captain.

April 23, 19--

Chief L. Gardner Langtree
Peoria Fire Department
3490 West Cumberland
Peoria, IL 61614

Dear Chief Langtree:

Roycemore Elementary School will present a Fire Safety Day on May 10. The program will run from 9:00 am to 12:00 noon. Our school has 170 students who range in age from 7 through 12 years.

We would like to have two firefighters from your department on hand throughout the program as speakers to talk to the students about fire safety. The speakers should cover fire prevention measures, how to report a fire, what to do if students are caught in a fire, and how to treat burns until help arrives.

We have scheduled a one-hour program planning meeting at 4:00 pm on May 5th at the school and would like your representatives to be present at the meeting. Please let me know if your department will be able to participate and who your presenters will be.

Thank you,

Dwayne C. Salven

Dwayne C. Salven
Principal, Roycemore Elementary School

SCHOOLS

The time children spend in school or school-related activities is critical to their growth and well-being. School systems, in turn, try to involve parents as much as possible in their children's education. As a parent, you can have considerable influence on programs; curriculum; selection of school board members, teachers, and principals; and quality of school facilities. An active parent-teacher partnership can help to guarantee a quality education for the community's youngsters.

Many parents hesitate to get involved because they don't know what they can do or whom they can write to with a concern or suggestion. The model letters in this section show ways that people can participate in their school system.

Requesting Parent-Teacher Conference

When your child is experiencing difficulties in school, your first step is to ask for a conference with his or her teacher. You can find out what the problem is and begin to work on ways to correct it. The teacher may be able to suggest outside help for your child or ways that you and the teacher can provide a better learning environment.

December 2, 19--

Dear Mr. Eddington,

I am concerned about the steady decline in Alice's math grades since fall. I know math has never been her best subject, but she seems to be having particular difficulty with algebra. Her last two test scores were near failing.

I would like to schedule a time when my wife and I can meet with you to talk about what can be done to bring up Alice's grades. Although it would be hard for us to afford a tutor, perhaps the school can provide extra help.

My wife will be out of town the rest of this week, so please call me at my work number (348-1600 ext. 435) to arrange a time when we can all get together. Thank you.

Sincerely,

Broderick Cooke

Broderick Cooke

Complaint About Teacher

Although parents are sometimes tempted to feel that the teacher is at fault if their children are having difficulty, there are times when a teacher genuinely *is* the problem. If you suspect this is the case in your child's class, consult with other parents before writing a letter. If you can write from a point of consensus, your complaint will carry more weight. Direct your letter either to the principal of the school or to the superintendent of schools in your district.

November 16, 19--

Ms. Jayne Hardesty
Principal
Eaton Elementary School

Dear Ms. Hardesty:

As parents of children in the sixth grade at your school, we are reluctantly writing you to protest the poor quality of math instruction the children are getting in Mr. Haines's class. Our complaint is based on several factors:

— Mr. Haines often steps out in the hall during class to talk with people who walk by.

— He assigns virtually no homework, while other math classes have homework every night.

— Although he leads class discussions about math, he fails to put problems on the board so that students can follow his steps in solving the problems.

— His tests are confusing, often leaving out essential information, or covering only the most elementary math skills.

Although the students like Mr. Haines, they complain that they are behind the other math classes and see little chance of catching up. This gap will hurt them even more when they move on to seventh grade and try to do more advanced work.

We are very concerned about this problem. Please either talk with Mr. Haines or consider replacing him before more of the year goes by. We will be paying for private tutoring, but many of the parents can't afford such help. They have a right to expect that the money they pay in taxes entitles their children to a good education.

Sincerely,

(Signatures of parents)

Complimenting Teacher

Let teachers know when you appreciate their abilities or extra effort they take with your children. Teaching is a demanding job, and one of teachers' rewards is knowing that they have made a difference in students' lives. Your letter can be sent either to the teacher, principal, or superintendent.

June 14, 19--

Mr. Anthony Peters
Superintendent of Schools
District #122

Dear Mr. Peters,

I wanted to let the 7th and 8th grade teachers know what a superb job they did setting up the Science Fair at Grace Middle School. Parents and children alike thoroughly enjoyed the event and learned a great deal besides. In particular, the liquid nitrogen display stole the show. My son and daughter have been talking about nothing else since Saturday.

For me, however, the real value was in the teachers' taking the time to show the children how to present their work in a nearly professional manner. The kids learned how to write a proposal, submit progress reports on their projects, write up a final paper, and put on a demonstration. I know Ruth and Eddie worked hard on their projects and felt a real sense of accomplishment after the Fair was over.

Please tell all the teachers how much we appreciate their efforts. Such events make us proud to be part of this school.

Sincerely,

Ashton and Lydia Kemmer

Appeal to School Board

When you have a concern that requires a change or addition to curriculum or school programs, writing the school board is an appropriate first step. The school board oversees school curriculum and programs and has the authority to change or establish existing policies. Be as specific in your letter as possible, outlining your idea or concern and what you believe can be done about it. Direct your letter to the president of the school board.

November 3, 19--

Mrs. Pilar Villa-Lobos
President, School Board
City Hall
Cary, IL 60012

Dear Mrs. Villa-Lobos:

The recent state policy of combining learning-disabled children with normal children in the public schools has created a real problem in the classrooms. Our son, who is dyslexic, attends Cary-Grove High School in district 23. Because of his problem, he has a difficult time keeping up with other students in the class. I know the same is true for other children who are learning-disabled.

I would like the school board to establish a learning disabilities program at our school. There is a model LD program already set up at Woolridge High School in district 152 that is working successfully. I understand the director, Dr. Robert Yates, has helped other school districts establish similar programs in their schools.

Please take care of this matter. The children with learning disabilities are not only falling farther behind in their schoolwork but are often the butt of other students' jokes. They should get help, not ridicule, from their schools.

Thank you.

Sincerely,

Leanna Strom

Leanna Strom

Notice of Absence

At times you may need to request that your children be excused from school because of family events. In your letter, make arrangements for your child to complete any assignments beforehand or to keep up with the rest of the class. A teacher's main concern will be that the child's learning schedule should not be sacrificed for family outings.

Dear Mrs. Kruse,

Our family will be taking a spring vacation to Washington, DC, from April 1 to April 10. Although this is no problem for our two older children, Southfork Middle School has its vacation from March 25 to April 1. Thus, Scott will miss a week of school from April 3 to 10.

We would like to know if Scott can do his assignments before we leave and if we could have a schedule of homework that he can take with him. Even though our trip is a tour of historic sites, we are concerned that Scott doesn't fall behind in his classwork.

Please call me at home 677-1907, evenings, to make arrangements for Scott's assignments. He is very excited about taking the trip and has already started reading about how many stairs there are to climb in the Washington Monument. We appreciate your help.

Yours truly,
Willard Nelson-Hunt

Excusing Student from Class Activity

When a student has been ill or injured and is returning to school, it may be necessary to limit his or her participation for a time. Let teachers know what the child should and shouldn't do. Be sure to include any doctor's instructions and emergency phone numbers where you or a doctor can be reached if necessary.

Dear Ms. Howard,

Please excuse Sara from any gym activity for the next two weeks. She is recovering from a particularly severe strain of flu virus and has already had one relapse by trying to come back too soon. I have enclosed her physician's instructions that she refrain from vigorous physical activity for two weeks.

Sara can still sit in on classes and attend the health and hygiene sections of gym class. After about two weeks, she should be strong enough to start moderate activity again. We appreciate your help in getting her back on her feet.

Sincerely,
Elizabeth Green

Appealing Admissions Board Decision

Some schools are well known for their specialties in vocational or technical training. If your child applies to such a school and is turned down, you can appeal the decision. In addition to talking with school officials, ask others who know your child's academic abilities and character to write to the school as well. The following model letter of appeal was written by a student's tutor.

May 30, 19--

Freshman Admissions Coordinator
Shawn Technical High School
2015 West Addison
St. Louis, MO 63108

Dear Mr. Kelleher:

It has come to my attention that Tom Mondala is appealing your decision regarding his application to Shawn Technical High School. I am writing in support of that appeal.

As a professional tutor, I have worked with many middle school students in math and science to prepare them for the transition to high school. I have been working with Tom since September and have been continually impressed by his willingness to apply himself and to overcome his weaknesses in chemistry. This effort in a subject area that is not his strongest indicates to me that he is the kind of student who would succeed at Shawn Technical.

As I have come to know Tom personally, I find he has a solid, outgoing nature with a strong desire to attend Shawn Technical. He is particularly talented at violin and wants very much to take part in the strong musical program at Shawn. He was clearly disappointed when his application was turned down, because he knows Shawn's music program is superior to those in other high schools.

I believe Tom will make an excellent and well-motivated student at Shawn Technical, one who will contribute richly to the school's music program and activities. I urge you to reconsider your decision and to accept Tom into your freshman class this fall.

Respectfully,

Norman C. Trevin, Ph.D.

Norman C. Trevin, Ph.D.
NCT Educational Consulting Services

Requesting Information from College/University

As high school students enter their senior year, they begin the search for a suitable college or university. You can help by showing them how to write for catalogs, bulletins, and other information from various schools. The public library has several references on hand to help you find correct addresses of schools and the contact person to write. Generally, you will address your letters to the Dean of Admissions or to the Office of the Registrar of a school.

Tell your child to mention any special interest he or she might have in a particular department or subject area. It may be that the school has special programs or advanced classes in that area.

November 10, 19--

Mr. R. B. Hutton
Dean of Admissions
Roosevelt University
3412 Little Ave.
Chicago, IL 60606

Dear Dean Hutton:

I am interested in attending Roosevelt University and would like to have a catalog, financial aid information, and other materials I might need to apply for the fall 19-- semester.

I am particularly interested in knowing about your Marine Biology Department. Could you send me the telephone number of the department's chairperson or one of the faculty members? I would like to talk with them about their marine biology programs.

I have a week's vacation at spring break, March 25–April 1, and would like to visit Roosevelt's campus. Are there any visiting programs for high school students?

Please send me all the information you can. I want to know as much about Roosevelt as possible so that I can apply soon. Thank you.

Sincerely,

Marianne Fleur-Villon

Marianne Fleur-Villon

Accepting or Declining Admissions Offer

Your child may be accepted by more than one school. He or she should put an acceptance or refusal in writing, either stating that he or she looks forward to attending the school or giving a reason for declining the acceptance offer.

June 6, 19--

Dear Ms. Logan,

I am very happy to learn that I have been accepted by the University of Iowa. The university was my first choice, and I am excited about starting in the undergraduate writing program. My parents are very pleased that I was awarded a writing scholarship and will have my tuition covered for the first year.

Enclosed is my housing application and deposit for the 19-- academic year. I will be able to attend the orientation session the first week in September. With senior finals out of the way, I am really looking forward to starting at the university in the fall.

Sincerely,
Albert Rookey

June 9, 19--

Dear Dean Forschen:

Thank you for your notice that I have been accepted at Coe College. I enjoyed meeting you and the other faculty members during spring break.

However, I have been awarded a full-tuition scholarship at the University of Iowa and have decided to accept the university's offer. I am very excited about attending the fiction writing workshops.

Thank you for your kind offer.

Truly yours,
Albert Rookey

SPORTS/YOUTH GROUPS

Sports leagues and youth groups (such as YMCA/YWCA, scouting, church clubs, and so on) are the most common activities parents and children engage in during the years children are growing up. These activities give children an opportunity to learn skills, develop socially, and have fun. However, sports and youth groups can also present problems if the people who organize and run them are not serving the best interests of the children.

If you have a compliment or concern, you can exercise your rights as a parent and write a letter to the appropriate officials, whether a coach, scout leader, commissioner of a sports league, or director of youth group activities.

Complimenting Sports Coach

Coaches are in a difficult position—squeezed between the desire to have a winning team and the expectations of parents that their children will play in every game. Yet a good coach can make a big difference in a youngster's life, particularly by instilling self-confidence in the child and improving his or her skills. If you have seen such development in your own child, let the coach know you appreciate what he or she has done.

> Dear Coach Sucaro,
>
> I'm writing to compliment you on your coaching of the Louisville Reds. My son Brayton is one of the players on your team. He has been playing in baseball leagues for three years, but this year he has been more enthusiastic about baseball than I have ever seen him.
>
> Although we appreciate the baseball skills you are teaching Brayton, we appreciate even more the role model you provide and the values you are teaching the kids. Brayton has really matured in the past six months, and I believe that part of it is due to your influence. Thanks for caring about our kids.
>
> Sincerely,
> Wade and Sharon Malone
>
> P.S. If you need extra help at the upcoming games, let us know.

Requesting Removal of Sports Coach

If a coach's style or manner becomes a serious problem, the parents can request that he or she be removed. In Little League, the letter would be written to a commissioner or head of a board of directors. If the coach is managing a park district or school league, write the park commissioner or the superintendent of schools.

Although asking for a coach to be removed is a drastic step, it may be in the best interests of the children. State clearly why you believe the individual should be asked to step down, and be prepared to talk to the commissioner or a board of inquiry who will investigate the matter.

September 27, 19--

Pauline Deel
Commissioner, Lakeview Park District
City Hall
Lakeview, OH 43331

Dear Ms. Deel:

It is with regret that we ask you to remove Ms. Lynda Myers as coach of the girl's Blue Division soccer team. The parents are agreed that her abrasive manner is ruining the sport for the girls involved. Many of them refuse to go to practice anymore, and nearly a third have dropped out altogether. Something needs to be done quickly or the entire Blue Division team will disappear.

We recognize that Ms. Myers has great technical skills—she was one of the top women soccer players in the country, and we considered ourselves fortunate to get her as coach. But she has little ability to control her temper and often lashes out at the girls for even small mistakes. She kicks over benches, throws equipment, and shouts at the top of her lungs at every game—and even during practice sessions.

Her decisions during the game are also hurting the kids. She will yank someone out for even minor mistakes and make her sit out the rest of the game. The children's enthusiasm for the sport has taken a sharp nosedive. We did not enroll our children to have them spend game time feeling guilty for missing a kick or having a ball stolen by an opponent.

We would like to set up a meeting with you next week to discuss this matter. The parents are willing to talk with you at your convenience. Many of us have tried to talk with Ms. Myers but to no avail. Please contact me at 445-3287 to discuss a time and place when we can meet.

Sincerely,

Georgia Waters
Georgia Waters

Youth Group Leadership

Youth groups can be a valuable experience in children's lives, teaching them skills, community responsibility, and social values. However, much depends on the leadership, which is often supplied by volunteers.

If you have a complaint about a group or club leader, contact the organization's local director. Most nationally organized youth activities have district or regional offices. For Boy Scouts or Girl Scouts, for example, you can write to the field director about the problem. The scouting council is the next step, followed by the regional office and national headquarters. Individuals at these levels generally are paid staff members and may be able to ask a group leader to step down and to reorganize the group under a new leader.

A good youth group leader, like a good coach, can be a strong role model for children. If your group has such a leader, let that person know how much you value his or her contribution to your child's growth and development.

September 9, 19--

Dear Mr. Jackson,

Just a note to say what a great job I think you're doing with the Y Explorers. You have had to handle some pretty rough problems over the past year, and I think the kids are stronger for it — I know my son Jason is.

The near-drowning of one of the boys on a camping trip shook up everyone, and the way you handled the children's feelings helped them deal with the incident. I know it had been preying on Jason's mind. After your sessions, he felt much better.

I've talked with the other parents, and they also appreciate your skill with the children, teaching them not only the activities they like — camping and climbing hills — but also values to help them make decisions. You would be interested in how often Jason uses the phrase, "Mr. Jackson says . . ."

Keep up the good work — we single mothers especially appreciate someone with your abilities as a leader. If I can help out at any of the meetings or special events, please let me know.

Sincerely,
Lilith Cousins

≡EIGHT

EMPLOYMENT LETTERS

Employment letters are those in which you apply for a job, request a letter of reference or write one, accept or refuse a position, acknowledge the help of others in your job search, and resign from a position. During your working life you will need to write one or more of these letters. Knowing how to write effective employment letters can help you to compete successfully in the job market.

Your first job search generally comes after you have completed your schooling. By that time, you have identified some of your interests, abilities, and skills, and you are searching for an entry-level position. As you gain experience in the working world, your job search is likely to change. You may want to switch fields, advance your career, or find a more challenging position.

BEGINNING A JOB SEARCH

Where do you begin your search process? It depends on what stage in your career you find yourself. Beginners may discover the most leads from school placement offices, while more experienced workers may get recommendations from friends in the field. The following are some of the more fruitful resources to help you find the best position.

1. *School placement offices*. If your school has a good reputation for providing occupational training and support for graduates, you may have a wide range of job leads to pursue. Your teachers may be able to give you additional leads or put you in contact with people working in your chosen field.

2. *Classified and company ads*. Employers advertise openings in newspapers and journals to attract qualified candidates. These ads may request a letter of application and your résumé, or a phone call to set up an interview.

   If you have experience in your field, you may want to confine your search to professional publications or company newsletters that advertise job openings. Many manufacturing and light industry firms also have job billboards outside their plants advertising openings for skilled and unskilled workers.

3. *Employment agencies.* State and private employment agencies also help to match up job candidates with openings. State agencies are free of charge.

Private employment agencies charge either the applicant or the employer for successfully matching a candidate with a job. Some companies prefer to work through employment agencies, because the agency's prescreening process ensures that only qualified candidates will be referred for interviews. Applicants can be sure that only jobs matching their qualifications and backgrounds will be recommended.

4. *Professional groups and associations.* Although the first three job sources work in many cases, they are part of the "numbers game," in which you comb through a list of opportunities and eliminate the unsuitable ones. As you gain experience in your field, however, you will build a network of contacts that can help you locate new positions. Joining a professional group or association in your field is one way you can move up the professional ladder.

5. *Personal referrals and recommendations.* This method is by far the most successful in locating new jobs. When you let people know you are searching, you activate your job network. Others will pass on information about job openings. Because they know you, they tend to recommend only those jobs that are suited to your personal qualifications and needs.

6. *Civil service and institutional offices.* Job openings in civil service at the federal, state, county, and city levels are also excellent employment opportunities. Various levels of government regularly publish notices of positions available. If you are interested in such a career, contact your local government employment office for information about applications and civil service exams.

In addition, hospitals, colleges, universities, churches, volunteer associations, civic groups, and other institutions have business offices that employ messengers, maintenance people, warehouse and shipping workers, mail room and office clerks, typists, secretaries, managers, and others. If you would like to work outside the traditional business field, you might consider one of these institutions.

7. *Individual companies.* Many companies do not actively recruit candidates through classified ads or employment agencies. Applicants can apply directly to the human resources (personnel) office of the company and inquire about job openings. Even if there is no immediate job opportunity, your application or résumé can be placed on file for future reference.

In larger companies, the turnover rate is sometimes high, and the personnel office is constantly recruiting and hiring new employees. If you contact these firms directly, you may find your call coinciding with an opening in the company. At the least, you have contacted the firm and made your qualifications and interest known.

RÉSUMÉS

There are many excellent resources on how to prepare a résumé available in the public library or in book stores. In addition, many search firms, employment agencies, and career counselors can show you how to put together an effective résumé. Figure 8.1 shows a sample résumé for someone looking for a management position.

There are no hard-and-fast rules regarding résumé layout or content. However, every résumé should display your name, address, and telephone number; work experience; education; and a note that references will be furnished on request. Some résumés also feature a brief line about the position or career objective the candidate is seeking, or a line about interests. Employers may find it useful to know what additional interests or skills a candidate possesses.

Your résumé, along with your query or application letter, presents you to a prospective employer. You should take time to make both documents look as professional and clear as possible.

Figure 8.1 Sample Résumé

Lillian Sample
1435 North Shore Drive
Chicago, Illinois 60611
(312) 328-7743

Position
Sought: Buyer for major retail clothing store.

Experience: *Assistant*
            Buyer   Carroll's Red Hanger Shop
            1986–present   566 North State, Chicago, IL 60606

            Responsible for ordering all men's
            ready-to-wear clothing and accessories.
            Handled budgets up to $250,000. Increased
            sales 20 percent in two years. Supervised
            three assistants and one secretary.

            Sales Clerk   Geske's Clothes
            1984–1986   34 Virginia Street, Urbana, IL 61801

            Handled all sales transactions in men's and
            boys' wear. Responsible for special orders
            and customer relations.

Education: B.A. in business and marketing, June 1984,
            University of Illinois, Champaign-Urbana, IL

Honors: Edwin Ebert Marketing Award, 1983–1984
         Delta Tau honorary business society, 1982
         AID Scholarship, 1981

Activities: Vice President, Delta Tau, 1983–1984
            Big Ten Marketing Exhibit, organizer, 1983

References: Mr. Harold Walker   Mrs. Leslie Geske
            General Manager   Owner
            Carroll's Red Hanger Shop Geske's Clothes
            566 North State   34 Virginia Street
            Chicago, IL 60606   Urbana, IL 61801
            (312) 445-7384   (217) 459-6533

            Other references furnished upon request.

Figure 8.2 Sample List of References

```
               JOHN P. CORVINO
    1001 Brown Ave., Evanston, IL  60202
              (708) 222-7150
```

```
                   REFERENCES
```

Work-related references   *Educational references*

LUCITRON, INC.   NORTHWESTERN UNIVERSITY

Alan Smith (manager)   Dr. Michael Rivers
Vice President, Operations   Thesis Advisor
Lucitron, Inc.   Electrical Engineering
1918 Richmond Drive   and Computer Science
Northbrook, IL 60062   Evanston, IL 60201
(708) 475-8364   (708) 452-8834

Jeff Williams (supervisor)   Dr. Shri Joshi
Research Engineer   Professor of Engineering
AMOCO Research Center   Marquette University
P. O. Box 500   G6   Electrical Engineering
Naperville, IL 60566   Department
(708) 328-7711   2315 West Argyle Ave.
                                             Madison, WI 43992
                                             (414) 422-1584

                                             Casey Krist
BIO-IMAGING RESEARCH, INC.   Senior Research Director
                                             Northwestern University
Dr. Nand Gupta (supervisor)   Electrical Engineering
Engineering Manager   and Computer Science
Bio-Imaging Research, Inc.   Evanston, IL 60201
438 Burser Drive   (708) 452-6904
Lincolnshire, IL 60069
(708) 543-9003

MOTOROLA, INC

Angie Epstein (supervisor)
Manager of Product Engineering
Motorola, Inc.
Communications Division
4332 Edgewater Drive
Franklin Park, IL 60131
(708) 452-3000 X4678
```
```

JOB QUERY LETTER

In a job query letter you are inquiring about job openings in a firm or institution. A résumé accompanies your query letter, showing the employer your experience and qualifications. You can also include a list of references that the employer may contact (Figure 8.2 shows a sample list of references). The employer may place your letter and résumé on file and call you when an opening occurs, or he or she may ask you to reapply when a vacancy is advertised.

You lose nothing by sending a query letter, and you may gain an interview, either right away or several months later. The important factor is that you are letting people in the field know who you are and what you can offer. One job seeker was contacted by a company nearly a year after he had sent the original query letter. He was offered and accepted a new position.

Before you write your query letter, research the company or institution. Show the recipient that you know something about the organization's business, and state what type of position you are looking for. Remember to include your résumé and, if you like, a list of references the employer can contact.

July 17, 19--

Barbara Feldenkrist, Director
One-to-One Learning Center
183 Lakeview
Suite 123
Northfield, IL 60093

Dear Ms. Feldenkrist:

Recently, I learned of the activities of your tutoring center and have been impressed with the work your organization is doing with middle and high school students. I am a tutor in math, science, and computers and would be interested in talking with you about working with One-to-One Learning Center. My resume and a list of references are enclosed.

I have taught basic physics, math, and computer science at the high school and middle school levels. Also I have done private tutoring both here and in New York City for over four years.

Tutoring and teaching have always been enjoyable for me. I like the opportunity to share my skills and to help young people overcome learning disabilities and obstacles. Perhaps you might need a tutor with my background and skills.

I look forward to hearing from you.

Sincerely,

Althea Davis, Ph D

Althea Davis, PhD
458 Hinman
Lake Forest, IL 60045
(708) 334-2187

APPLICATION LETTER

An application letter is written to apply for a specific position. The main purpose of the letter is to catch the interest of a prospective employer and help you secure an interview. Employers read application letters to weed out candidates who are obviously unsuitable and to select the few they will interview.

Since your letter of application is the employer's first introduction to you, think carefully about how you want to present yourself. What do you want the letter to say about your qualifications, work experience, and abilities? Make sure your letter is written on bond paper and is free of erasures, strikeovers, misspellings, and other errors.

Address the letter to a specific person. Call the company or institution to find out who will be receiving the letter. This tells the reader that you took the time and effort to research the job opening. If you have only a box number to write, address the letter "Dear Sir or Madam."

The application letter must capture the recipient's attention and focus on how your qualifications meet the needs of your prospective employer. Begin your letter by stating what position you are applying for and what experience, if any, you have had:

Dear Mr. Huston:

Please consider this an application for the position of delivery-man for your main warehouse on Front and Third streets. For the past three summers, I have worked as a deliveryman for Oakes Manufacturing.

If you have learned of the vacancy through a friend, relative, employee of the organization, or other individual, it may be to your advantage to mention the person's name (provided you have permission).

Ms. Carla Norris, your sales manager, told me that you were looking for a corporate communications manager. I have been senior editor at Watson and Co. for five years and would enjoy a chance to apply my skills to help produce your company's publications.

Once you have established how your qualifications match the employer's need, you can support your case in the middle paragraphs. Keep your letter brief and focused. Highlight aspects of your educational background and business experience that relate directly to the job you are seeking.

At Motorola, I supervised the work of four technicians and three process engineers working on high-tech consumer products. I was responsible for all quality testing and performance standards checks and had final authority to approve shipment or halt production of any product. My team achieved an overall performance rating of 98.1 percent.

Your final paragraph should tell the reader what action you want taken. In the application letter, you want the reader to give you a personal interview. Make your request easy to grant.

I'd welcome the opportunity to discuss my qualifications for this opening. Can we arrange for an interview? I can be reached at 433-5621 before 9:00 A.M. or after 6:00 P.M.

Remember, the purpose of the application letter is not to tell the whole story of your work history but only to convince the employer to grant you an interview. The interview is the time to discuss your skills and experience in more detail. Look over the sample letter of application below.

September 18, 19--

Dr. F. Robert Boscamp
Northern Scientific Company
1123 Melrose Drive
Hopkins, MN 55343

Dear Dr. Boscamp:

I am responding to your advertisement in the Sunday Star-Tribune placed under both the education and engineering categories. This dual listing intrigued me, as my experience has been strong in both teaching and in industry. Also, I have long admired your company's consumer product line.

While obtaining my PhD, I taught physics and electrical engineering at the University of Minnesota for three years. Since that time I have been working at Gould Electronics as a process engineer involved with inspection, qualification, and upgrading materials on a product assembly line. My latest project has been supervising work on a prototype color flat-panel display unit. I also continue to teach one course a semester in the University's physics department.

The details of my education, work history, and publications are given in the enclosed resume. I would enjoy an opportunity to meet with you and learn more about Northern and your program needs. Would it be possible to set an interview next week? I can be reached at 566-1907 after 6:00 P.M.

Respectively yours,

Chris Streeter

Chris Streeter
4930 Beard Avenue N.
Minneapolis, MN 55429

RECOMMENDATION LETTERS

During your career, you will probably write two types of reference letters: letters requesting recommendations or references *from* someone, and letters of recommendation written *for* someone else.

Requesting References

Employers often want to know something about the character, work habits, training, and experience of their candidates. You can ask others to act as references for you and supply their names, addresses, and telephone numbers on your reference list. Or you can ask your references if they will write a letter of recommendation to be sent either to you or directly to a prospective employer.

If you ask someone to act as a reference for you, include the following in your letter:

1. The specific position you are applying for

2. Reasons why you wish to use the individual as a reference

3. A stamped, self-addressed envelope for his or her reply

By telling your references the position you are seeking and why you would like to use them as a reference, you help them know in advance what questions a prospective employer is likely to ask.

A letter requesting permission to list someone as a reference might look like the following:

June 11, 19--

Dear Professor Skoda:

I am applying for the assistant sales manager's job at Quaker Oats in Chicago, Illinois.

Since I received my basic sales training and management experience in your class and assisted you in consulting to business firms, I would like very much to use your name as a reference.

I have enclosed a stamped, self-addressed envelope for your reply.

Sincerely,

Mary Elgar

A letter asking for a recommendation sent directly to the employer might read as follows:

June 11, 19--

Dear Professor Skoda:

I am applying for the assistant sales manager's job at Quaker Oats in Chicago, Illinois.

Since I received my basic sales training and management experience in your class and assisted you in consulting to business firms, I feel that you know my work style and business strengths better than anyone.

Would you be willing to write a letter of recommendation on my behalf to Ms. Fran Dyra, Vice President–Sales, at Quaker Oats? Enclosed is a stamped envelope addressed to Ms. Dyra for your convenience.

Sincerely,

Mary Elgar

Writing a Recommendation

At times you may be asked to write a letter of recommendation for a friend, former employee, or colleague. Your letter should include the following:

1. How long you have known the person

2. The nature of your relationship or acquaintance (boss, friend, teacher, colleague)

3. Your assessment of the person's qualifications, character, and work

Your enthusiasm about the candidate is reflected in the amount of detail you provide. A few, generalized statements will do for someone you know slightly or for the work record of a person you observed but did not directly supervise. On the other hand, explicit detail indicates that you believe the candidate has superior abilities. Employers usually appreciate knowing as much about candidates as possible.

The following is a strong letter of recommendation.

February 4, 19--

Representative Dawn Michaels
Capitol Building
Tempe, AZ 85281

Dear Ms. Michaels:

I heartily recommend Jake Tobin as an addition to your staff in Tempe. Jake has worked directly under me for three years in the Republican Party office here in Tucson. He started as a volunteer canvasser, moved to a paid staff position, and for the past year has been managing our local election campaigns.

Since Jake has worked in the statistics department at Market Facts, Inc., he also can help your staff analyze voter polls and election statistics. His expertise in this area should help you target specific voter groups or judge which issues should be emphasized in your campaigns. I believe his insights into voter attitudes and voting patterns will prove invaluable to you and your staff.

Jake is skilled both in number crunching and with people—a rare combination indeed. In fact, if Jake has any faults at all, it is in his tendency to provide so much information that you can get overwhelmed. I suggest that you tell him specifically what you need to know and give him strong guidelines.

I definitely recommend you hire Jake as an addition to your staff. You would be getting an exceptional worker.

Cordially,

Jillian C. Peters

Jillian C. Peters
Committeewoman, GOP

FOLLOW-UP LETTERS

Once you have secured an interview with a prospective employer, you should write a letter expressing appreciation for the time the person spent with you and the information about the job and company they shared. At this point you may also want to express your appreciation for any assistance you have received from friends, teachers, fellow employees, colleagues, and others.

Letters Following an Interview

If you have obtained an interview with an employer, you are one of a select group of candidates being considered for the job. The letter you write after the interview gives you the chance to:

1. Thank the interviewer for the time and courtesy shown you

2. Let the interviewer know of your continued interest in the job

3. Remind the interviewer of your qualifications for the position and how the company would benefit from your experience

4. Provide any additional data requested by the interviewer that you may need time to collect

5. Turn in an application form or other form you may have received to complete at home

September 13, 19--

Mr. Howard Branston
Vice President, Product Development
Tool Works, Inc.
Lincolnwood, WA 98014

Dear Mr. Branston:

It was a pleasure to meet with you and your staff at the new Tool Works facility in Lincolnwood. I was very impressed with your hydraulic equipment. Our talk gave me a clear picture about what you are looking for in a shop foreman.

I am more interested in the job since I had a chance to see your operations and learn what your goals for the division are. I believe that my experience as shop foreman at Boeing Aircraft has given me the background in heavy tooling machinery and supervisory responsibilities to help you meet those goals. I am particularly interested in your plans for converting from steel to plastics molding.

I am enclosing my job description, which you requested, and have asked my references to write letters of recommendation directly to you. I will forward the application form as soon as I return from Sacramento.

I hope that my qualifications meet your criteria for shop foreman at your new plant. If you need further information, I can be reached at 922-4378.

Sincerely,

Strom Kierjard

Strom Kierjard

Letters of Appreciation

Even before you accept a job offer, you may want to write letters thanking the people whose support, encouragement, and suggestions have helped you in your job search. A letter of appreciation is a brief note to your supporters mentioning their specific contribution and letting them know how you are doing.

April 7, 19--

Ms. Helen Gervais
JVS Vocational Institute
348 Claridge Road
Orlando, FL 32822

Dear Ms. Gervais:

This is to let you know that I have been offered positions by two companies since we last spoke. I just want to express my appreciation to you and the staff at JVS for all the assistance I received during the time I was laid off.

Your personal counseling helped me reevaluate my skills and attitudes and helped me see the type of work I really wanted to do. In particular, the videotaped interviews showed me how to handle myself under pressure. I never realized that I tugged at my jacket so much when I get nervous.

Also, your advice on how to write letters of application and prepare a resume helped me get interviews with three companies. I'll let you know the minute I land a full-time position. Keep up the good work—you are really needed out here.

Best regards,

Kyle Warren
Kyle Warren

ACCEPTING OR REFUSING A JOB OFFER

You've made it through the interview process, your references checked out fine, you like the company—finally you are offered the job. You still have a choice: to accept or refuse the offer. In either case, you need to put your choice in writing.

Acceptance Letter

If you decide to accept the offer, your letter constitutes a form of written contract. It should include:

1. A statement accepting the position

2. A brief paragraph restating why you believe your new employer made the right choice

3. A date when you can report for work

September 24, 19--

Dear Ms. Fiddle:

I am pleased to accept your offer of a senior editor position at Pergamum Books. You can be sure I will bring all my experience as an editorial and educational consultant to bear on this job. I believe that my general familiarity with your projects will enable me to make a smooth transition from consultant to full-time editor. I will be able to start Monday, October 1, as we discussed on the phone. I will report to the personnel office at 8:30 A.M. and to your office at 9:00 A.M.

Thank you for this opportunity. I look forward to working with you and the rest of the editorial staff in the College Division.

Sincerely,

Michael B. De Foe

Michael B. DeFoe

Refusal Letter

You might refuse a job offer for several reasons. Perhaps you've received a better job offer or realized you are not really suited for the job. Whatever the reason, you should respond to the job offer with a tactful, friendly letter of refusal. You want to maintain good communication—some time, you may wish to reapply at the company.

Use the diamond sequence for your refusal letter, expressing appreciation for the offer and giving your reasons for turning the offer down.

July 19, 19--

Dear Mr. Porthus:

I appreciate the offer of a secretarial position at Island Lake Exports. The benefits and salary are among the best I've seen anywhere.

However, as we discussed, the job would mean driving two hours a day to and from Island Lake. After careful thought, I have decided to take a position as a secretary at Hywood Manufacturing here in Gurston. Although this job is less attractive than the one with your firm, it's much closer to my home and family.

I appreciate the time you spent with me. I know there are many good candidates who can fill your position.

Sincerely yours,

Maureen Thompson-Hayes

Maureen Thompson-Hayes

LETTER OF RESIGNATION

During your career you may need to write a letter of resignation when you leave a job. You may find a better position, plan on going back to school, or have a serious clash with your supervisor.

Whatever the reason, your letter of resignation should be courteous and positive. You may want to use your former employer as a reference. Letters of resignation, like letters of refusal, follow the diamond sequence.

August 1, 19--

Dear Mr. Hightower:

I have enjoyed working with you and the staff at the League for Urban Renewal. These past two years have been among the most rewarding in my career life.

However, our work with local community groups has inspired me to return for my master's degree in social work. I appreciate now how valuable such a degree can be in my field of endeavor. I would like to start school in the fall, and would appreciate it if you would accept my resignation, effective September 15.

I will be able to stay on through the summer and help you find a replacement for my position. Thank you for all the patience, wisdom, and experience that you shared with me. I will always remember my time with the League with great affection, and hope to work with you and the staff again in the future.

Sincerely yours,

Antonio Verranzo
Antonio Verranzo

CHILDREN'S LETTERS

Children can begin learning at an early age how to write letters. The ability to express themselves well in writing is a skill that will prove invaluable in their social and career lives.

However, forcing children to write "duty" letters to relatives or friends, or being too critical of their first efforts, can teach children to dislike letter writing. Letters written under such conditions often convey little, if anything, of the child's natural feelings.

As a parent, teacher, or adult friend, you can do a great deal to foster good letter-writing skills in children. Show children that writing, like speaking, is a form of dialogue. Your first opportunity may come when children ask the all-too-common question, "What should I write about?"

This chapter presents some techniques and guidelines for helping children learn *and enjoy* letter writing, whether for required thank-you notes or for messages to family members, friends, VIPs, pen pals, celebrities, or others.

LETTER-WRITING TIPS FOR CHILDREN

The following suggestions can help you prepare children to write good letters. Be available to answer their questions and to review their first efforts.

1. *Provide them with special writing materials and a special correspondence drawer or space.* Let them pick out their own stationery, perhaps with their name or initials. Keep correspondence materials in a special place that encourages children to do nothing but write letters in that place.

2. *Encourage writing thank-you letters and other notes as a family activity.* It is easier, particularly for young children, to write letters if it is done as a group activity. Holidays are an appropriate time to teach letter-writing skills. You can get your own thank-you letters done at the same time, setting a good example for your children.

3. *Have children write their thank-you notes or other letters while the emotion or experience is still fresh.* Children tend to live in the moment, and an experience of a day or two ago is hard to recapture. Have them write their notes while they are still enthusiastic about the gift, visit, or other experience.

4. *Allow children to express themselves in their own words.* Even though you might be able to think of the perfect phrase or wording, let your children say things for themselves. Much of the charm in receiving letters from children is in the unique way they see things.

   However, exercise some discretion in this area. If your child starts out the letter with "My mom made me write this thank-you letter," you can use your editorial privileges and delete the sentence.

5. *Avoid being overly critical about spelling, grammar, and other mechanics.* Although children need to learn good grammar skills, don't focus on these aspects to the detriment of a child's spontaneity. Sometimes such "errors" can add unexpected humor or interest to their letters.

6. *Don't take over the task if the children dawdle or stall.* Writing for some children is hard work, and they will try to get you to take over the task. Start out by letting them write short letters, maybe a line or two, and praise them for completing the messages. Once they realize they can't trick you into writing letters for them, they will learn to do it themselves.

7. *Get children's senses involved and get them excited about communicating something to someone.* If children run out of ideas or seem unwilling to think for themselves, get their senses involved. Ask them what they would like to tell a relative or friend—how does that activity or item feel, smell, taste, sound, or look?

   If their grandfather is interested in birds, for example, what birds can the child see from the window? What are they doing? What would the grandfather be interested in knowing about the birds around the child's house? This line of thought not only activates children's creativity but gets them to think about the reader's interests and needs as well.

8. *Finally, cultivate good letter-writing habits in yourself.* Your example is the most powerful teacher your children have. They will watch you to see how you write letters, when you write them, and what your attitude is about letter writing. If you procrastinate yourself but scold them for not writing promptly, your example will speak louder than your words. On the other hand, if you enjoy letter writing, that enthusiasm is likely to transfer to your children.

The following sections provide model letters for a variety of situations in which children will need to communicate appreciation, sympathy, or news about themselves; ask for information or advice; and express opinions and concerns.

THANK-YOU NOTES

Children will find it easier to write thank-you letters soon after they receive a gift or return from a party or visit. Their emotions are still focused on the item or event, and they will be able to recall what they appreciated or liked.

The sample letters below are written by children ranging in age from seven to thirteen.

Gifts

Encourage children to mention specifically the gift they were given by the person they are writing and what in particular they liked about it. If they didn't like the gift or feel neutral about it, suggest that they simply write "the gift was very nice" or "thank you for picking out the gift for me." This approach helps them recognize the giver's intentions even if the gift falls short of the mark.

Dear Aunt Nelly and Uncle Frank,

Thank you for the bear you sent. I like it a lot. I got watercolors and a wood train set for my birthday. I call the bear Kevin. I can take his coat off when it is hot.

Will you come see us? Kevin wants to see you, too.

Love,
Sarita

Dear Toshi,

Thank you very much for the book about Indians. The pictures are neat — especially the ones that show the Plains Indians. My Dad says he can help us build a tepee in the back yard.

It was too bad you had to miss my party. We played this new computer game, "Revenge of the Empire." When you come over, I'll show you how it works.

Thanks for the book — I'm almost done with it.

Get well,
Brian

Hospitality

Like adults, children should learn to write "bread-and-butter" letters to thank their hosts after a visit. If the child visited a friend, the friend's parents should also be thanked, either in the same letter or in a separate letter.

Dear Angie,

I had a super time at your house, especially horseback riding. Next time let's stay for two hours! Can you believe how many horses that stable had?

Mom says we can have an overnight at my house next weekend. Ask your mom if you can stay Friday or Saturday night. We could make a campfire out back. Do you want to ask Frieda or Chandi to come over too?

Anyway, thanks again for the weekend. I had a great time!

Your friend,
Joan

Dear Mr. and Mrs. Wallenberg,

Thank you for having me over to your house. Angie and I really loved the horseback riding. I hope we didn't smell too much like horses when we got back in the car.

Can Angie come over to my house next weekend? I would like her to stay either Friday or Saturday night.

Mom and Dad say hello, too. I told them how pretty Angie's room looked. Thank you for a wonderful time.

Sincerely yours,

Joan

INVITATIONS

Party invitations can range from the highly imaginative to a simple fill-in notecard. Children like to be involved in creating invitations, and even the youngest can help fill in a name, address, or date and time of the party.

When your children receive invitations, make sure they note any special instructions on the invitation and help them devise ways to remember the party dates—for example, tacking the invitation on their bulletin boards or on the refrigerator door.

Sending Invitations

For young children, the printed, fill-in invitations are easiest. The children can add their own colors or figures to decorate the note paper. Older children can either create their own invitations or simply write a note to the people they want to invite.

Accepting Invitations

In many cases, you will not need to send a note of acceptance to a child's invitation, just take your child to the party. However, an acceptance note is always welcome and teaches young children the courtesies of social life. Parents can write acceptance notes for very young children; otherwise, encourage your children to write their own. When your child is invited by the parents of a friend, have them write the acceptance note to the parents.

Dear Brian,
    I'll be coming to your party on Saturday — baseball and pizza, who would miss it? This is going to be one fine party.
    I'll see you there!

                  Zeke

Dear Mrs. Ramachandra,
    Thank you for inviting me to go on the trip with you and Pavli. It sounds like a wonderful vacation, and I know Pavli and I always have a good time together.
    My parents have said I could go, and they will be calling you to talk about the details.
    I'm really excited about seeing Colorado. Thank you very much for asking me.

                  Sincerely,
                  Brittany

Declining Invitations

If your child cannot attend a function, make sure a note of regret is sent. Have your child explain briefly why he or she cannot go and close with best wishes for a successful party or outing.

Dear Shirl,

I got your invitation for your camping weekend. It sounds like a lot of fun, and I'm really disappointed that I can't come. The doctor said I couldn't put any weight on my ankle for another week. Bummer! I'll be on crutches until the 14th.

I hope you all have a super time. I can just see Cindy tramping through the woods looking for a drug store at night. Tell me about it when you get back.

Love,
Luci

PERSONAL CORRESPONDENCE

When teaching children to write letters to family, friends, pen pals, and personal heroes and heroines, encourage them to write as they speak. Give them suggestions for the content of their letters:

► Describe their surroundings

► Describe their friends—who they are and what they do

► Tell about something surprising, scary, exciting, boring, or unusual that happened recently

► Mention what other family members are doing

► Talk about their sports, hobbies, school classes, outside activities, trips, movies, or other aspects of their lives

► Describe their pets and any tricks or quirks the pets have

► Mention new skills they have learned or would like to learn

► Ask about their recipient's interests, surroundings, family, friends, and so on

Family

Most letters to parents or other family members from children will be written when children go away to camp or are away on a trip or vacation. If you are a parent waiting for a letter from a young camper, don't expect long, detailed messages. Children are usually too involved in what is going on to write at any length.

However, you can encourage children to write informative letters. Talk to them beforehand about what makes an interesting letter, and provide them with stationery and self-addressed, stamped envelopes. In your own letters to them, avoid asking questions that have a "yes" or "no" answer ("Do you like the camp?" "Is your roommate nice?" "Have you gone swimming yet?"). Instead, ask questions that will elicit more detailed answers ("What are you learning at camp?" "What did you do on your first day?" "Which camp counselors do you like the best?").

When children write other family members, encourage them to go over the list of ideas for letters. Avoid forcing them to write "duty" letters. Such messages are apt to sound stilted, insincere, and uninspired. Instead, try to get them excited about communicating something about themselves to the relatives.

Dear Mom and Dad,

Camp Echo is full of mud right now. It rained two days. We have to play inside. They say we can see a movie tonight. Stan is in the bunk below me, and he brought all his comic books. Sometimes we read with a flashlight at night.

I sure hope we can go swimming soon. They have a big pool with rubber rafts in it. Are you coming to see me this Saturday?

Love,
Ricky

Friends

In addition to the usual friendship letters, you can suggest to your children that their friends might appreciate a letter when they are ill, in the hospital, going through a hard time (parents are divorcing or there has been a death in the family), or other occasion. Children can generally be more frank with one another than adults can often be, particularly about matters of death or illness.

Encouraging children to write such letters can help to foster empathy and sensitivity in their relationships with others.

Dear Evie,

I noticed that you looked really sad in gym class today. I just wanted to say that I know how bad it feels to have your folks split up. Mine did last year, and I felt awful. My stomach hurt all the time. Mom finally took me to the school counselor, and that helped.

Anyway, I just wanted to let you know that I understand if you don't feel like talking to anybody. I sure didn't. If you want to go to the movies this Saturday, let me know. We can stop at that new snack shop - the one with the cookies. If you don't have any money, I can pay. I get my allowance on Thursday. Sometimes you just need your friends.

Angie

Pen Pals

Pen pal correspondence, particularly with children from other countries, offers another opportunity for children to communicate not only as themselves but as representatives of their country and culture. Foreign pen pals can help a child understand that people view the world through widely different lenses.

You can help your children correspond more effectively by encouraging them to learn about their pen pals' countries and customs. If a pen pal asks questions your child may not know how to answer, help your child investigate the questions. The experience, even if it lasts for only a few months, can be a memorable one for your child.

Dear Shaki,

I was glad to get your last letter. It sounds like it gets really hot in Delhi in summer. Here in Seattle it hardly ever gets that hot, and it's always raining off and on. We have one of the world's only temperate rain forests. I wish you could see it - and the mountains. Did you get the pictures I sent in my last letter?

You wanted to know how come a rich country like ours has homeless people. I asked my Dad, and he said it's a tough problem. He says we're working to make things better for them. Our church has a soup kitchen in the basement, and Dad says we can feed almost 100 people a day there. Oh, a soup kitchen is really just a regular kitchen that has food for people who don't have any money to buy food themselves.

In your letter you said you were Hindu. Do you have a holiday like Christmas, where you give presents? Do you have to go to religious classes to learn about Hinduism in your church or temple? I'm going to religious classes now. We have to memorize all the books of the Bible. I looked up Hinduism in the encyclopedia - you have almost as many gods and goddesses as we have saints! I was named after Saint Jerome, but nobody calls me Jerome. It's usually Jerry or Jer.

I wish you could come to visit us in Seattle. We could go skiing in the mountains. That's my favorite sport. What do you play? Do they have basketball there? I'm a Seattle Sonics fan and go to a game every chance I get.

I hope your family is well. Tell me more about what you do in India and what it's like. Maybe someday I can come there.

Your friend,
Jer(ome)

Fan Letters

Children often develop crushes on authors, music or sports stars, or other celebrities and may wish to write to them. Your child may wish to write to a celebrity. The celebrity may even respond, which is always thrilling to a child.

You can find the addresses of many celebrities by writing to major recording companies or movie studios or to sports team offices. Authors can be reached by writing to them in care of their publishers. Also, check with the public library. They may have such resources as *The Address Book: How to Reach Anyone Who Is Anyone,* by Michael Levine (Perigee Books, a Putnam Books Division, 1988). The book contains the addresses of over 3,500 notable people.

Encourage your child to tell the recipient what he or she likes about the individual or about the person's work, how it makes the child feel, and any requests the child would like to make. Be sure children understand that the celebrity may not respond, but that writing the letter to express their thoughts and feelings is worthwhile.

Dear Miss Jordan,

I just finished reading your twelfth mystery book— Behind the Golden Door —and I wanted to let you know how much I like your books. I'm 11 years old and I want to be a detective when I grow up. I think it's important to start learning how to observe people and pick up clues early.

I especially like your main character, Amanda Drake. She always sees things other people miss, like the time she noticed the suntan mark on the guard's right wrist, though he said he was right-handed. It was a clue that he was really left-handed. Also, she seems like a good friend. I felt really sad when her friend's mother died and Amanda took her friend home with her. My friend Jackie and I are like that.

One thing I wanted to ask. In <u>Behind</u> <u>the Golden Door</u>, on page 22, you say the doctor left his black bag in the car. On page 25, though, he reaches into his bag to get his bottle of medicine. How did the black bag get from the car into the house?

Please write more Amanda Drake stories. Can you do one where she goes on the space shuttle and has to prevent it from being sabotaged? How about one set in Brazil or in the Middle East? You are my favorite author, and I hope you write many, many more books.

Sincerely,
Justine Horton

OTHER LETTERS

Children may be required to write letters related to schoolwork, to exploring careers, or in regard to some social issue they are learning about. You can help your child focus their letter on a specific issue or topic.

Requesting Information

When children must write to agencies, companies, or individuals to ask for information, help them determine exactly what they need to know. For example, "Send me all your information on wild animals in North America" is too broad a request. Get them to narrow the topic down—what kind of animals, what do they need to know about them? "Send me information on the habitat of cougars in the United States" is much more manageable. A trip to the library can help locate the proper agency, company, association, or person for them to write.

April 10, 19---
Mr. Robert F. Civgin
Managing Director
Riverside Nuclear Power Plant
Riverside, CA 94332

Dear Mr. Civgin,
   My sixth grade class is doing a report on nuclear power safety. Could you please send me information on the safety precautions Riverside Nuclear Power Plant takes against nuclear accidents?
   What do you do if someone finds a leak or discovers radioactivity outside the plant? Can you shut the plant down? I am very interested in nuclear power, so I want to know all I can.

Thank you for your help.
Sincerely,
Suzanne Choi

Asking for Advice

At times your child may need to ask the advice of someone more experienced about a project, problem, or skill they want to explore. The person may be a relative or friend of the family, but he or she also may be a celebrity or well-known public figure. Suggest to your child that he or she list the things he or she wants to know, and then pick one or two of the most important items. People are more likely to respond to one or two well-phrased questions than to five or six general queries.

Dear Mr. Frankl,

I am very interested in raising golden retrievers. My parents said I could have a retriever puppy if I take care of it and train it. My Dad said you raised golden retrievers when you were in Georgia.

I would like to know how much it costs to raise and train one golden retriever. What is the best kind of food for it? When should I start training the puppy?

I would be glad to get any advice you can give about raising these dogs. I hope to have a kennel of my own someday. I love retrievers and have wanted one ever since I can remember.

Thank you for your time.

Sincerely,

Gerald Wheatley

Writing VIPs

If your child becomes concerned or involved in an issue such as environmental pollution or animal rights, he or she may ask you how to write to the president of the United States, a federal or state representative, the heads of corporations or companies, or other VIPs. Your child may want to express concern or compliment the VIP on some action taken or statement issued.

Such involvement should be respected. If children are writing a compliment, encourage them to state specifically what they liked. If it is a concern, help them express their feelings in a firm but tactful way. Stress that they will be taken more seriously if they refrain from name-calling, threats, demands, or other manipulations.

Correct titles and forms of address for many public figures are provided in Chapter 4.

May 13, 19__
President of the United States
White House
1600 Pennsylvania Avenue
Washington, D.C. 20500

Dear Mr. President,

I learned on TV last week that chemical companies have been dumping their garbage near my town. The show said that other companies have been dumping garbage in other towns.

I think you should try to stop this. This is poisoning the ground and the water, and we have to live here and eat and drink this poison. The show said that a lot of kids were getting sick because of this.

Please help us get rid of these chemicals. Maybe we could shoot them out in space or send them into the sun. We have to do something before this poison kills everything around here. We can't use our river anymore because there are so many dead fish.

A concerned seventh-grader,
Troy Jeska

APPENDIXES

EASILY CONFUSED WORDS

accept, except

> *accept*—(verb) to take, agree
> I *accept* your apology.
> *except*—(adverb) excluding, omitting
> She remembered everything *except* the plane ticket.

advice, advise

> *advice*—(noun) opinion, counsel
> She needs legal *advice* about her accident.
> *advise*—(verb) to counsel someone about something
> Her lawyer *advised* Maria to sue the cab company.

affect, effect

> *affect*—(verb) to influence, change
> His decision will *affect* his entire future.
> *effect*—(noun) impression, results; (verb) to cause
> The recession had a profound *effect* on our town.
> It *effected* a complete change in our downtown area.

already, all ready

> *already*—(adverb) even now
> Do you believe it's February *already*?
> *all ready*—(adjective) all prepared
> They are *all ready* to go to Europe.

assent, ascent

> *assent*—(verb) to agree; (noun) permission
> She *assented* to his request.
> You need your cousin's *assent* to bring an extra guest.
> *ascent*—(noun) advancement
> They made their final *ascent* on the hill this afternoon.

capital, capitol

> *capital*—(noun) wealth; seat of government
> We need *capital* to start up our business.
> Let's visit the state *capital* this year.
> *capitol*—(noun) government building
> The tornado damaged the *capitol*'s roof last night.

cite, site, sight

cite—(verb) refer to, state; to serve notice on

My accountant *cited* three reasons why I should start an IRA.

Our landlord was *cited* five times for failing to install smoke alarms.

site—(noun) location

On this very *site* your grandfather started his first hardware store.

sight—(noun) scene

The brilliant fall trees are a stunning *sight*.

cloths, clothes

cloths—(noun) pieces of cloth

We used velour *cloths* to polish the silverware.

clothes—(noun) wearing apparel

I'm giving all my old *clothes* to the rummage sale.

complement, compliment

complement—(noun) something that completes

Her practicality is a perfect *complement* to his imagination.

compliment—(verb) to say something good about someone; (noun) a flattering remark

Mother *complimented* Julie on her physics prize.

The *compliment* obviously meant a lot to Julie.

consul, council, counsel

consul—(noun) foreign embassy official

We had to see the German *consul* about our passports.

council—(noun) official body

Sam is writing a proposal for the city *council* to consider.

counsel—(verb) to advise; (noun) legal advisor

Is anyone *counseling* you about your claim?

Maybe my lawyer will act as your *counsel* in court.

dissent, descent, descend

dissent—(noun) disagreement

Our councilman cast the only vote in *dissent* of the measure.

descent—(noun) a decline, fall

My bank account experienced a steep *descent* in March.

descend—(verb) to come down

We can have the bride *descend* from the balcony staircase.

fewer, less

fewer—(adjective) lower in number (used for individual units, numbers)

Tran had five *fewer* donuts today than he had yesterday.

less—(adjective) reduced amount (used for quantities)
This car has *less* headroom than last year's model.

formerly, formally

formerly—(adverb) previously
Nancy Chang, *formerly* Nancy Sun, just had a baby.
formally—(adverb) officially
Kyle was *formally* sworn in as Kiwanis president last night.

imply, infer

imply—(verb) to suggest
Are you *implying* that I ate your chocolate cake?
infer—(verb) to deduce from evidence
From the chocolate smears on your hands and face, we can *infer* that you
ate the cake.

it's, its

it's—contraction of *it is* or *it has*
I don't know if *it's* (it is) Wednesday or Thursday.
It's (it has) been a confusing week.
its—possessive form of the pronoun *it*
The car just dropped *its* muffler in the street.

later, latter

later—(adverb) after a time
Call me *later* today; I'll be out this morning.
latter—(adjective) the last mentioned of two items
We have two choices: Pittsburgh or New York. I'll take the *latter*. I always
loved New York.

lay, lie

lay—(verb) to put or place something (lay, laid, laid)
Where did you *lay* the napkins? I *laid* them on the table. Someone must
have laid something on top of them.
lie—(verb) to rest or recline (lie, lay, lain)
I'm going to *lie* down for awhile. You *lay* down just an hour ago. In fact,
you *have lain* around the house all morning.

lead, led, lead

lead—(verb) to go before, to conduct; (adjective) first
Howard is going *to lead* the seminar Saturday. His daughter Chantae is the

lead speaker for the panel.
led—(verb) past tense of lead
I *led* the horse into the stable.
lead—(noun) heavy metal; graphite
Score your test with a *#2 lead* pencil.

lose, loose, loss

lose—(verb) to misplace
Every winter I *lose* one of my gloves.
loose—(adjective) not fastened down; (adverb) release
The *loose* hinges on this door need to be tightened. Let's turn the kids *loose* in the yard.
loss—(noun) deprivation
Your cousin's death must be a great *loss* to you.

passed, past

passed—(verb form) went by, gone by
Once on the highway, we *passed* every car in sight. We *passed* up a chance to stop at the roadside museum.
past—(adjective) preceding
Over the *past* four years the town has changed a great deal.

personal, personnel

personal—(adjective) individual, private
I want to tell you something very *personal* about myself.
personnel—(noun) department or division; workers
Paula got a job in *personnel*. She knows all the *personnel* in the company by now.

precede, proceed

precede—(verb) to come before
In the *preceding* week, we sold four hundred boxes of Girl Scout cookies.
proceed—(verb) to go ahead, to initiate
I think we can *proceed* with ordering more boxes of cookies.

principal, principle

principal—(adjective) main, foremost; (noun) superintendent
My *principal* concern is for the girls' safety. The school *principal* has assured us the trip is well planned.
principle—(noun) rule, standard
One *principle* of parenthood is be flexible!

quiet, quite

quiet—(adjective) silent

Since the boys left, things are too *quiet* in the house.

quite—(adverb) completely; to a considerable degree

I *quite* agree that car insurance rates are too high. When I received the current bill, I was *quite* upset.

rise, raise

rise—(verb) to go up; (noun) reaction

We watched the moon *rise* last night. Mention politics and you'll always get a *rise* out of Ed.

raise—(verb) to lift, to bring up; (noun) an increase

The Martinellis had to *raise* their house on its foundations. I hope Carla's *raise* in pay can cover this expense.

set, sit

set—(verb) to put or place something

Should I *set* the vase on the bureau?

sit—(verb) to rest or recline

After walking six hours, I couldn't wait to *sit* down.

stationary, stationery

stationary—(adjective) still, fixed

The carpenters took out everything but the *stationary* beam.

stationery—(noun) letter paper

I got six boxes of personalized *stationery* for my birthday.

than, then

than—(conjunction) after a comparison

Jody is now taller *than* his father.

then—(adverb) next, in that case; (noun) that time

If you don't like that college, *then* transfer this spring.

By *then*, you'll get your first semester grades.

that, which

that—(conjunction) used to introduce a clause that contains information essential to the meaning of the sentence.

We bought the Victorian house *that* has the white gables. (*that has the white gables* tells which Victorian house among many it is)

which—(conjunction) used to introduce information generally not essential to the meaning of a sentence

We bought a Victorian house, *which* has white gables, on Grove Street.
(*which has white gables* is incidental information)

their(s), there, they're

their(s)—possessive form of *they*
Which house is *theirs*? I didn't bring *their* address.
there—(adverb) indicates a place
Is it *there* on the corner?
they're—contraction of *they are*
The house looks dark; I wonder if *they're* home.

weather, whether

weather—(noun) climate
If you don't like the *weather* here, just wait a minute—it will change.
whether—(adverb) if; regardless
Do you know *whether* Helen is coming? We'll have to leave soon *whether*
she comes or not.

who's, whose

who's—contraction of *who is* or *who has*
Who's (who is) going to the concert? I don't know *who's* (who has) been
invited.
whose—possessive form of who
Whose orange hair dye is this?

you're, your

you're—contraction of *you are*
You're not going to believe what I saw.
your—possessive form of *you*
I saw *your* son, and he's dyed his hair orange.

COMMONLY MISSPELLED WORDS

A

abbreviate
absence
abundant
accessible
accommodate
accompanies
accompaniment
accumulate
accuracy
acknowledgment
acquaintance
adequately
admission
admittance
adolescence
adolescent
advantageous
allege
alliance
analysis
analyze
anonymous
apologetically
apparatus
apparent
appreciate
appropriate
argument
arrangement
ascertain
association
attendance
authorize
auxiliary
awfully

B

ballet
bankruptcy
beneficial
bibliography
bookkeeper
boulevard
brochure
buffet
bulletin

C

calculation
calendar
camouflage
cancellation
catalog
catastrophe
category
cellar
cemetery
changeable
choose (present tense)
chose (past tense)
colossal
column
commitment
committed
committee
comparative
compatible
competent
competition
competitor
complexion
conceivable

concise
conscientious
consciousness
consensus
consistency
contingency
controlling
controversy
correspondence
correspondent
criticism
criticize
curriculum

D

debacle
debt
debtor
decadent
deceit
deceive
deference
deferred
dependent
depreciation
description
desirable
detrimental
dilemma
diligence
disastrous
discrimination
dissatisfaction
division
divisive

E
economical
ecstasy
effect
efficiency
efficient
embarrassment
emphasize
endeavor
enforceable
enormous
enthusiastically
entrance
espionage
exaggerate
excel
excellent
exceptionally
exhaustion
exhibit
exhibition
exhibitor
exhilarate
exhilaration
existence
exorbitant
expensive
extension
exuberant

F
facilitate
facilitator
familiar
familiarity
familiarize
family
fascination
feasible
feminine
foreign
franchise
fraud
fraudulent

freight
fulfill

G
gauge
grammar
grief
grievance
grieve
guarantee
guaranty
guidance

H
harassment
hereditary
hinder
hindrance
horizontal
hygiene
hypocrisy
hypocritical
hypothetical

I
ideally
idiomatic
illegible
immediately
imperative
implement
incidentally
inconvenience
indemnity
independent
indispensable
inevitable
inflationary
influence
influential
ingenious
initial

initiate
initiation
initiative
innocent
inoculate
institution
intellectual
interfere
interference
interpretation
interrupt
interruption
invoice
irrelevant
irresistible
itemize
itinerary

J
jeopardize
jeopardy
judgment

K
kerosene
knowledge
knowledgeable

L
labeled
laborious
legitimate
leisurely
liability
liable
license
likelihood
liquor
livable
loose
lose
loss
lucrative

luxurious
luxury

M
magistrate
magnificence
magnificent
maintain
maintenance
majestic
malicious
manageable
mandatory
maneuver
marketable
materialism
measurable
mediator
mediocre
melancholy
metaphor
miniature
miscellaneous
mischievous
misspell
misstatement
mortgage
mosquito
municipal
mysterious

N
naive
naivete
necessary
negligible
negotiate
neurotic
neutral
ninety
ninth
noticeable

O
objectionable
observant
occasionally
occupant
occurred
occurrence
omission
omitting
opinionated
option
outrageous
overrated

P
pageant
pamphlet
parallel
prophesy
prove
psychology
pursuant
pursue

Q
qualitative
quality
quantify
quantitative
quantity
questionnaire
quietly
quit
quite

R
rebellion
rebellious
receipt
receive
recommend
recommendation
reconcile

reconciliation
recur
recurrence
reducible
reference
referred
rehearsal
reimburse
reimbursement
relief
relieve
reminiscent
remit
remittance
remitted
repetition
representative
resource
respectfully
responsibility
returnable
reveal
revelation
revenue
routine

S
salable
schedule
scientific
scrutinize
scrutiny
separation
sergeant
serviceable
siege
significant
similar
similarly
souvenir
specifically
specimen
sponsor
statistics

strategic
stubbornness
substantial
succeed
succession
superficial
superfluous
superintendent
supersede
supervisor
suppress
surroundings
susceptible
symbolic
symmetrical
synonymous

T
tariff
technical
technician
technology
temperature
tendency
theoretical
tolerance
tolerant
tomorrow
traffic
trafficking

tragedy
tragic
transcend
transmit
transmittal
transparent
tried
twelfth
tyranny

U
unanimous
undoubtedly
uniform
universal
unknown
unmistakable
unnatural
unnecessary
unscrupulous

V
vaccination
vaccine
vacuum
variation
variety
vehicle
vengeance
ventilation

versatile
vigilance
vigilant
villa
villain
vinegar
volume

W
waive
waiver
warrantee
warranty
whisper
whole
wholly
withhold

Y
yacht
yawn
yield
young
youth

Z
zealot
zealous
zenith

POSTAL ABBREVIATIONS

DIRECTIONS

North	N	Northeast	NE
East	E	Southeast	SE
South	S	Southwest	SW
West	W	Northwest	NW

STATES, TERRITORIES, AND POSSESSIONS

Alabama	AL	Missouri	MO
Alaska	AK	Montana	MT
American Samoa	AS	Nebraska	NE
Arizona	AZ	Nevada	NV
Arkansas	AR	New Hampshire	NH
California	CA	New Jersey	NJ
Canal Zone	CZ	New Mexico	NM
Colorado	CO	New York	NY
Connecticut	CT	North Carolina	NC
Delaware	DE	North Dakota	ND
District of Columbia	DC	Ohio	OH
Florida	FL	Oklahoma	OK
Georgia	GA	Oregon	OR
Guam	GU	Pennsylvania	PA
Hawaii	HI	Puerto Rico	PR
Idaho	ID	Rhode Island	RI
Illinois	IL	South Carolina	SC
Indiana	IN	South Dakota	SD
Iowa	IA	Tennessee	TN
Kansas	KS	Texas	TX
Kentucky	KY	Utah	UT
Louisiana	LA	Vermont	VT
Maine	ME	Virginia	VA
Maryland	MD	Virgin Islands	VI
Massachusetts	MA	Washington	WA
Michigan	MI	West Virginia	WV
Minnesota	MN	Wisconsin	WI
Mississippi	MS	Wyoming	WY

STREETS

Alley	ALY	Heights	HTS
Avenue	AVE	Highway	HWY
Beach	BCH	Island	IS
Bend	BND	Islands	ISS
Bluff	BLF	Junction	JCT
Boulevard	BLVD	Lake	LK
Branch	BR	Lakes	LKS
Bridge	BRG	Landing	LNDG
Burg	BG	Lane	LN
Bypass	BYP	Lodge	LDG
Canyon	CYN	Manor	MNR
Cape	CPE	Meadows	MDWS
Center	CTR	Mission	MSN
Circle	CIR	Mount	MT
Court	CT	Mountain	MTN
Courts	CTS	Parkway	PKY
Cove	CV	Place	PL
Creek	CRK	Plaza	PLZ
Crescent	CRES	Point	PT
Crossing	XING	Port	PRT
Dale	DL	Prairie	PR
Drive	DR	Ridge	RDG
Estates	EST	River	RIV
Expressway	EXPY	Road	RD
Falls	FLS	Spring	SPG
Ferry	FRY	Springs	SPGS
Forest	FRST	Square	SQ
Forge	FRG	Station	STA
Fork	FRK	Stream	STRM
Forks	FRKS	Street	ST
Fort	FT	Summitt	SMT
Freeway	FWY	Terrace	TER
Gardens	GDNS	Trail	TRL
Gateway	GTWY	Turnpike	TPKE
Glen	GLN	Valley	VLY
Grove	GRV	Viaduct	VIA
Harbor	HBR	View	VW
Haven	HVN	Village	VLG

I N D E X